Other Publications:

THE ENCHANTED WORLD
THE KODAK LIBRARY OF CREATIVE PHOTOGRAPHY
GREAT MEALS IN MINUTES
THE CIVIL WAR
PLANET EARTH
COLLECTOR'S LIBRARY OF THE CIVIL WAR
LIBRARY OF HEALTH
CLASSICS OF THE OLD WEST
THE GOOD COOK
THE SEAFARERS
WORLD WAR II
HOME REPAIR AND IMPROVEMENT
THE OLD WEST
LIFE LIBRARY OF PHOTOGRAPHY (revised)
LIFE SCIENCE LIBRARY (revised)

For information on and a full description of any of the
Time-Life Books series listed above, please write:

Reader Information
Time-Life Books
541 North Fairbanks Court
Chicago, Illinois 60611

*This volume is one of a series that traces the adventure and
science of aviation, from the earliest manned balloon ascension
through the era of jet flight.*

AMERICA IN THE AIR WAR

by Edward Jablonski

AND THE EDITORS OF TIME-LIFE BOOKS

TIME-LIFE BOOKS, ALEXANDRIA, VIRGINIA

Time-Life Books Inc.
is a wholly owned subsidiary of

TIME INCORPORATED

FOUNDER: Henry R. Luce 1898-1967

Editor-in-Chief: Henry Anatole Grunwald
President: J. Richard Munro
Chairman of the Board: Ralph P. Davidson
Corporate Editor: Jason McManus
Group Vice President, Books: Joan D. Manley

TIME-LIFE BOOKS INC.

EDITOR: George Constable
Executive Editor: George Daniels
Director of Design: Louis Klein
Editorial Board: Roberta R. Conlan, Ellen Phillips,
Gerry Schremp, Gerald Simons, Rosalind Stubenberg,
Kit van Tulleken, Henry Woodhead
Editorial General Manager: Neal Goff
Director of Research: Phyllis K. Wise
Director of Photography: John Conrad Weiser

PRESIDENT: Reginald K. Brack Jr.
Senior Vice President: William Henry
Vice Presidents: George Artandi, Stephen L. Bair,
Robert A. Ellis, Juanita T. James, Christopher T. Linen,
James L. Mercer, Joanne A. Pello, Paul R. Stewart

THE EPIC OF FLIGHT

EDITOR: Dale M. Brown
Senior Editor: Jim Hicks
Designer: Raymond Ripper
Chief Researcher: W. Mark Hamilton

Editorial Staff for *America in the Air War*
Picture Editor: Jane N. Coughran
Text Editor: David S. Thomson
Writers: Adrienne George, Laura Longley,
Glenn Martin McNatt, Victoria W. Monks
Researchers: LaVerle Berry, Barbara Brownell (principals),
Patricia A. Cassidy, Roxie France
Assistant Designer: Van W. Carney
Copy Coordinators: Elizabeth Graham, Stephen G. Hyslop,
Anthony K. Pordes
Picture Coordinator: Betsy Donahue
Editorial Assistant: Caroline A. Boubin

Special Contributors: Josephine Burke,
Katie Hooper McGregor

Editorial Operations

Design: Ellen Robling (assistant director)
Copy Room: Diane Ullius
Production: Anne B. Landry (director), Celia Beattie
Quality Control: James J. Cox (director), Sally Collins
Library: Louise D. Forstall

Correspondents: Elisabeth Kraemer-Singh (Bonn); Margot
Hapgood, Dorothy Bacon (London); Miriam Hsia, Susan
Jonas, Lucy T. Voulgaris (New York); Maria Vincenza Aloisi,
Josephine du Brusle (Paris); Ann Natanson (Rome). Valuable
assistance was also provided by: Wibo van de Linde
(Amsterdam); Lesley Coleman (London); Cheryl Crooks
(Los Angeles); John Dunn (Melbourne); Carolyn T. Chubet
(New York); Dag Christensen (Oslo); Mimi Murphy (Rome);
Traudl Lessing (Vienna).

THE AUTHOR

Edward Jablonski, historian and biographer,
is the author of more than 20 books, most
of them on aeronautical themes, including
Flying Fortress, Warriors With Wings and the
authoritative four-volume *Airwar.* He has
been an aviation enthusiast since boyhood
and is a member of the American Aviation
Historical Society.

THE CONSULTANTS *for America in the Air War*

Donald S. Lopez, who holds a master's degree in aeronautics from the California Insti-
tute of Technology, is Chairman of the Aeronautics Department of the National Air and
Space Museum in Washington, D.C. During
World War II, he became an ace flying P-40
fighters in China under General Claire Lee
Chennault. After serving with the Air Force
until 1964, he spent eight years as a systems
engineer on the Apollo-Saturn launch vehicle
and the Skylab orbital workshop before joining the Smithsonian Institution in 1972.

Robert C. Mikesh, Curator of Aircraft at
the National Air and Space Museum of the
Smithsonian Institution, was commissioned
as a pilot in the Air Force in 1950. During the
Korean War he flew B-26 Invaders on night
tactical bombing raids and won a Distinguished Flying Cross and the Air Medal with
two Oak Leaf Clusters. His special interest,
developed after long service in the Far East, is
Japanese aviation history, and he has published numerous articles and books about
the aircraft flown in the Pacific theater during World War II.

Library of Congress Cataloguing in Publication Data
Jablonski, Edward.
   America in the air war.
   (The Epic of flight)
   Bibliography: p.
   Includes index.
   1. World War, 1939-1945 — Aerial operations, American.
2. United States. Army Air Corps — History — World War,
1939-1945. I. Time-Life Books. II. Title. III. Series.
D790.J33   940.54'4973   82-5539
ISBN 0-8094-3343-5   AACR2
ISBN 0-8094-3342-7 (lib. bdg.)
ISBN 0-8094-3341-9 (retail ed.)

CONTENTS

Wings around the globe

When the Japanese attacked Pearl Harbor on December 7, 1941, the Army Air Forces had only 1,100 combat-ready planes. No one could have imagined then that within the next four years the AAF would become the mighty weapon commemorated in the paintings reproduced on this and the following pages, or that it would have the scope to engage in what its commander, General Henry H. "Hap" Arnold, described as a "global mission." Nevertheless, by 1944 the AAF had grown into 16 separate air forces stationed around the world, and its 1,100 planes had grown to nearly 80,000.

Supplying the crews and aircraft of this far-flung organization was a major American achievement. The number of separate items required to arm, service and repair the aircraft—everything from tiny bomb-release buttons to 500-gallon fuel tanks—mounted steadily. Approximately 80,000 items were listed in 1940; by 1944 they came to 500,000. Between January 1942 and August 1945, some 19 million measurement tons, or 760 million cubic feet, of supplies were conveyed overseas by ship. To assure a steady infusion of new aircraft, some 40,000 planes were flown to foreign bases before the War's end, while approximately 47,500, primarily fighters, journeyed by sea.

But even this technological juggernaut would not have been enough without the 2,400,000 men of the AAF and their ability to adapt to the rigors of their separate theaters. The Eleventh Air Force, stationed on Alaska's frigid Aleutian Islands, resorted to blowtorches to warm frozen engines. In North Africa, Ninth Air Force ground crews pasted paper over their fighters' cartridge chutes to prevent sand from jamming the wing guns. And half a world away in the Pacific, mechanics of the Fifth, Seventh and Thirteenth Air Forces found that storing spare parts in airtight containers kept the jungle humidity from rusting them before they could be used.

B-24s of the U.S. Fifteenth Air Force based in Italy dodge heavy flak after loosing their bombs on the oil refineries of Ploesti, Rumania, Germany's largest supplier of fuel. "For the roughest target of them all, Ploesti was it," said an American gunner. "We called it the graveyard of the Fifteenth."

On the bleak Aleutian island of Amchitka, American ground crews service P-40 fighters in subarctic temperatures. After the Japanese captured two other islands in the Aleutian chain, the Eleventh Air Force flew frequent sorties from Amchitka to prevent an enemy advance toward mainland Alaska.

Laborers in Kunming, China, unload supplies from a C-46 transport that has just flown the Hump, a perilous route from India across the 15,000-foot Himalayas. Maintaining the sole supply line to Allied forces in China, American pilots airlifted 650,000 tons of cargo over the Hump between 1942 and 1945.

Sweeping in low, B-25 bombers of the Thirteenth Air Force strafe the Indonesian island of Halmahera. In the hard-fought Pacific campaign, the Thirteenth lent support to the Allied invasion of some Japanese-held islands and neutralized others so that invasion would be unnecessary.

Heavily laden with bombs, B-17 Flying Fortresses of the Eighth Air Force take off from an airfield in the English countryside. The largest American air force in World War II, the Eighth staged more than 260,000 bombing missions against targets in Germany and occupied Europe.

A dark cloud billows above Hickam Field, Hawaii, as recently delivered B-17 Flying Fortresses, parked on the runway the morning of December 7, 1941,

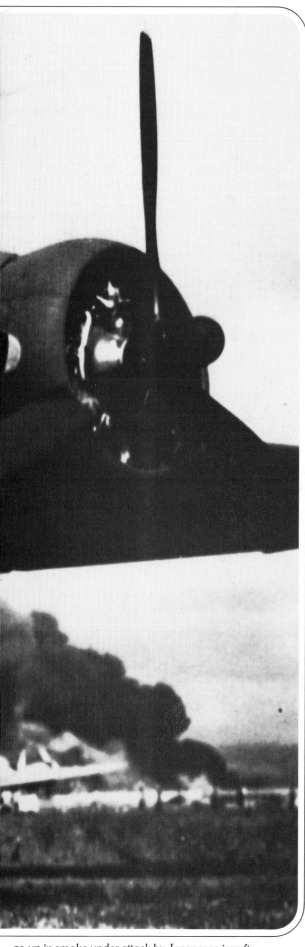

go up in smoke under attack by Japanese aircraft.

1

The fall and rise of U.S. air power

The six factory-fresh Boeing B-17 Flying Fortresses had begun their approach to Oahu in the Hawaiian Islands. After nearly 14 hours in the air, they were due to refuel at Hickam Field, just southeast of the naval base of Pearl Harbor, a halfway stop between California and their destination, Clark Field in the Philippines. The time was 7:50 a.m., the day—December 7, 1941.

As the big Fortresses got closer to Oahu, heading south and slightly west, a few alert crew members noticed groups of small planes in the air. They were not Army or Navy aircraft; with their fixed landing gear they looked as though they might be civilian craft. Some of the men thought that an honorary escort had been sent to greet them.

As flight leader Captain Richard H. Carmichael began his descent, he saw that the air over Hickam Field was unusually congested and that, ominously, thick columns of oily smoke curled upward from several of its buildings. Something was very wrong at Hickam. Rather than land there, Carmichael headed for Wheeler Field, a fighter base about 13 miles to the north. His wingman, Lieutenant Harold N. Chaffin, followed.

But the other four B-17s, dangerously low on fuel after their 2,400-mile transpacific trip, were forced to try to land at Hickam. Three made it down, despite the fire from wheeling fighters and Hickam's antiaircraft batteries. The crews, strafed from above by the attackers, ran for cover. None had ever seen the swift, single-engined monoplanes before, but the red circles—the Rising Suns—on the wings and fuselages identified them as Japanese. The Americans would soon learn that the strange aircraft were Mitsubishi Zeros, the best fighters then in the Pacific.

The fourth B-17, with Lieutenant Frank P. Bostrom at the controls, pulled away from Hickam's antiaircraft fire only to be set upon by six Zeros. Bostrom's Fortress, like all the others, had no machine guns or ammunition—they had been removed so that the B-17s could carry extra fuel. His only option was to dive the big bomber to treetop level, hedgehop to elude the Japanese and land his Fort on the first piece of clear ground he saw, which turned out to be a golf course.

Meanwhile Carmichael and Chaffin had discovered that Wheeler Field was also ablaze with destroyed pursuit planes and buildings. They flew northward until they spotted a tiny fighter field at Haleiwa and safely dropped their B-17s on its minuscule strip. So far six big Forts had managed to land with—miraculously—no casualties.

Now a second flight of six B-17s from the United States appeared over Hickam. Four landed there during a lull in the fighting, but the last two ran head on into a second wave of Japanese bombers and fighters. Zeros ignited the flares stored in one plane's radio compartment, sending the plane to earth burning furiously, and so shot up the other that its pilot, Robert H. Richards, fled eastward until he reached another fighter field, Bellows. The runway was too short for the big bomber, but with two of the crew seriously wounded, Richards took the plane down. He soon ran out of runway and skidded into the underbrush, where the landing gear snapped and the Fortress came to a stop on its belly.

The destruction of these last incoming B-17s — and the damage suffered by others — was only one of the blows inflicted on U.S. forces by the Japanese that fateful morning. In less than two hours 350 Japanese aircraft flying from six carriers that had sailed undetected to within 200 miles of Hawaii had not only crippled the American Pacific Fleet, but also knocked out some two thirds of Hawaii's Army planes. When the attack was over, fewer than 80 of the 231 operational aircraft assigned to the Hawaiian air force were flyable.

This brilliantly conceived and executed attack—the brain child of Japan's leading air-power advocate, Admiral Isoroku Yamamoto— came as a violent shock to most Americans. It was not a total surprise, however, to the American armed forces, although they were caught badly off guard at Pearl Harbor by Japan's unexpected ability to mount such a long-range air strike. The U.S. Army and Navy had in fact been gearing up for war—though not nearly fast enough, as it turned out—since 1938.

In that year President Franklin D. Roosevelt, alarmed both by Adolf Hitler's fast-rearming Germany and a Japan whose ruling military clique had already invaded China, urged Congress to vote increased funds for defense. Much of the money appropriated in 1938 went to enlarge the Navy, but in 1939, after further pleas by the President, Congress passed bills allocating about half of the year's military budget—the then Gargantuan sum of $300 million—to the Army Air Corps.

The money was badly needed. The Air Corps, like the Army, of which it remained a branch, had been starved for funds for two decades. Although an air service had been built up swiftly after the United States entered World War I in 1917, it was dismantled with equal haste after the 1918 Armistice. In 1922 America's air establishment numbered only 952 pilots and other officers and about 9,000 enlisted personnel. As a combat arm, it had effectively been demobilized.

Stringent military budgets throughout the 1920s and early 1930s— the American public, repelled by the 1914-1918 War, had become anti-military and isolationist—kept the Air Corps short of planes, personnel and often fuel. Even as late as 1938 the Air Corps was "practically nonexistent," according to the man who became its wartime chief,

A remnant of a B-17 caught on its approach to Hickam Field by strafing Japanese Zeros stands burned out on the tarmac. The plane descended in flames intact but broke in half upon hitting the ground. All but one of the crew survived.

General Henry H. "Hap" Arnold, especially when compared with the large air fleets then being constructed by Germany, Italy and Japan. The 1938 Air Corps could boast only some 19,000 men. Every plane being flown by the few active squadrons was obsolete, with the sole exception of the B-17. This beautiful aircraft would prove one of World War II's outstanding bombers. But by 1938 the Air Corps had taken delivery of only 13 of these appropriately named Flying Fortresses from the Boeing Company, with another 29 on order.

The $300 million shot-in-the-arm voted by Congress in 1939 enabled Arnold, a cherubic-looking but hardheaded and farsighted officer, to at last begin building a modern air force. He speeded the development of fast, heavily armed fighter types such as the twin-engined Lockheed P-38 and the rugged, single-engined Republic P-47. (The *P* stood for pursuit plane, a dated term for fighter. The P designation was nevertheless retained for Army fighter types throughout the War.) Arnold also encouraged the Consolidated Aircraft Company to hasten the production of another four-engined bomber, the B-24 Liberator. And in 1940 he persuaded Boeing to begin designing a successor to the B-17, a "Superfortress" that would become the B-29, by far the War's largest combat aircraft.

Despite his belief in the need for long-range, four-engined bombers, Arnold and his staff also hastened development and production of a generation of smaller, twin-engined aircraft that were designed to provide tactical support for the Army's ground forces: the light, swift Douglas A-20 (*A* for attack) and a pair of medium bombers, the North American B-25 Mitchell and the Martin B-26 Marauder. The result, Arnold wrote after the War, was the "best balanced air force in the world," capable of both the long-range strategic bombardment of an enemy nation's industrial base and ground-support missions.

The force Arnold commanded when war broke out, however, was not well balanced, well equipped or anywhere near large enough to fight a global conflict. As Arnold was well aware, it takes years to design a new aircraft, build a prototype, test-fly it, remove the bugs and then get an improved model into large-scale production. The B-24, which had been designed in 1938, did not reach combat squadrons in any numbers until 1942, and the story was similar for the P-38, the P-47 and the other new aircraft. In December of 1941, Arnold had only 1,100 planes fit for war service, and many of these, especially the fighters, would barely pass the test of combat. It took skill to turn the heavy Curtiss P-40's principal virtue, its fast diving speed, to advantage in combat with the swifter and more agile Japanese Zero or the German Messerschmitt 109. The Allison engine of the Air Forces' other combat-ready fighter, the Bell P-39 Aircobra, could not lift the plane to the altitudes commonly used by Japanese bombers.

During the first year of the War, the men of the newly rechristened Army Air Forces, or the AAF, had no recourse but to hold on grimly with inadequate equipment while the training schools and the U.S. aircraft industry hurried desperately to produce the planes and skilled personnel necessary to fight two different air wars in two vast and far-distant theaters, Europe and Asia.

Produce they did. The Air Forces' training system, which had been turning out some 300 pilots annually by 1939, was to be expanded to train 50,000 pilots each year by mid-1942. Dozens of new training fields were laid out and constructed all through the nation, and especially in the South and Southwest, where the weather offered better year-round flying conditions.

The aircraft manufacturers, furiously building new assembly plants and running old ones with three round-the-clock shifts and the help of a newly tapped labor supply, women, jumped production from a normal prewar 2,000 planes a year to 4,000 a month by late 1942. The Air Forces, which possessed a total of 1,700 planes in early 1939, would in the years 1940-1945 accept delivery of a staggering 229,230 aircraft. By 1945 the Air Forces numbered 2.4 million men.

While Arnold thus turned to account two American specialties, mass production and mass education, he could also call on a remarkable nucleus of able officers who had stuck with the struggling Air Corps through the lean years of the 1920s and 1930s with their faith in the military value of air power undimmed. Like Arnold—who had been taught to fly by the Wright brothers in 1911—these veteran Army aviators had grown up with the airplane and were intimately aware of what it could, and could not, do. Carl A. "Tooey" Spaatz and Ira C. Eaker had set endurance records in the previous decades, proving the airplane's abilities to stay aloft for long periods and to cover great distances. James H. Doolittle had become famous for setting speed

A mighty weapon's slow birth

When World War I ended, the U.S. Army Air Service, as the air force was then known, consisted of about 10,000 biplanes, most of which were soon sold or scrapped. "Not a dollar is available for the purchase of new aircraft," a 1920 government report flatly stated, and for the next 10 years airmen flew in obsolete—and accident-prone—craft. In a single year nearly 100 fliers were killed or seriously injured in 330 crashes.

But in 1926, when the Air Service was renamed the Air Corps, Congress authorized a five-year expansion program designed to bring the strength of this neglected branch of the Army up to 1,650 officers, 15,000 enlisted men and 1,800 planes. For the first time, the corps gained control over its own research and development funds.

Although the Depression slowed appropriations to a trickle, some important gains were made. Major training bases were built at Randolph and Kelly Fields in Texas. Specialists were called upon to plan for the future. And advances in aircraft construction and design began to catch up with the dreams of the few visionaries who all along had been championing air power.

Fabric-covered biplanes such as the P-12 (top right) gave way to sleek monoplane fighters. In 1932, the Martin B-10 (bottom right), touted as the world's most advanced medium bomber, appeared. In 1934 work began on a heavy bomber, the famous B-17 (far right). At last the country seemed to be showing the determination to have, as General Henry "Hap" Arnold put it, "airpower that you could put your hands on."

Boeing P-12s, last of the Army's biplane fighters, fly in line-abreast formation over Selfridge Field, Michigan, in 1932.

The Martin B-10 bomber was a clean all-metal monoplane with retractable landing gear whose top speed of 213 mph made it faster than most contemporary fighters.

A new B-17 arrives at Langley Field, Virginia, in March 1937 to undergo service testing. Nearly 13,000 of these heavy bombers would be built during World War II.

records, making the first coast-to-coast flight in less than 24 hours and the first blind flight, wholly on instruments. All three proved to be forceful air generals, able to translate their long experience of flying into effective command of the growing Air Forces' large combat units.

All three, like Arnold, had also absorbed the doctrine preached in the 1920s by America's apostle of air power, Brigadier General William "Billy" Mitchell, that fleets of heavy bombers could, in Mitchell's words, destroy an enemy's "means of making war" by hitting his "centers of production of all kinds." This belief in strategic air power dictated overall U.S. air strategy in World War II, and fortunately it was a belief shared by other members of the close-knit fraternity of between-wars Army aviators—among them George C. Kenney, Hoyt Vandenberg, Haywood S. Hansell and Curtis LeMay—who became in time commanders of one or another of the 12 separate combat air forces that Arnold had set up by 1945 to fly and fight around the globe.

But putting this long-range strategy into effect depended on planes and air crews, and at the beginning of America's involvement in the War both were in short supply. The AAF's tiny forces in the Pacific could do little to hold back the inevitable Japanese advance toward the oil, rubber and other essential commodities in Burma, Indochina and the Dutch East Indies. A vital steppingstone in Japan's path was the Philippines—then a U.S. possession—and there, only hours after the Pearl Harbor attack, the Army Air Forces' pitifully small outposts suffered another catastrophe. This time, however, the AAF units were not taken by surprise, as they had been in Hawaii. The cause of the debacle could be traced to human failings and misunderstandings.

General Douglas MacArthur, commander of all of the U.S. Army units in the Far East (as well as the Philippine Army), summoned the head of the Far East Air Force, Major General Lewis H. Brereton, shortly after news of Pearl Harbor reached Manila at 3:30 a.m. on December 8 (the Philippines are across the International Date Line from Hawaii). When Brereton arrived at MacArthur's headquarters he saw MacArthur's protectively loyal chief of staff, Brigadier General Richard K. Sutherland, whose ingrained distrust of the Air Forces as an upstart and unreliable branch of the Army exceeded even that of his superior.

Exactly what happened next has been clouded in controversy ever since. According to Brereton's published diaries, he requested permission to load bombs on the 18 B-17 Fortresses he had at Clark Field, the major Army air base on the northernmost Philippine island of Luzon, and stage a preemptive raid on the Japanese airfields dotting southern Formosa (now Taiwan). (Brereton's remaining 17 Fortresses had been flown to the uncompleted Del Monte Field on the island of Mindanao, 550 miles to the south, out of reach of Formosa-based Japanese bombers.) Sutherland, Brereton later maintained, refused to let him see MacArthur but promised to pass on Brereton's request and quickly relay MacArthur's decision. Brereton recalled that he then waited impatiently

JAMES H. DOOLITTLE

for orders—which did not come until it was too late. Sutherland, for his part, claimed that Brereton and MacArthur had discussed the wisdom of making the attack—and that holding the B-17s at Clark Field had been largely Brereton's decision.

The upshot was that Brereton mounted no assault on Formosa during the early hours of December 8, when Japanese planes, waiting for the morning fog to disperse over Luzon, were sitting on their airfields, vulnerable to attack. Brereton did, however, order his fighters

Appointed in June 1941 as Chief of the newly reorganized Army Air Forces, Lieutenant General Henry H. "Hap" Arnold (right) was made responsible for the establishment of Army aviation policies and plans. This organizational effort, aided by the officers below, all of whom had overseas commands, greatly increased the effectiveness of the AAF.

IRA C. EAKER

CARL A. SPAATZ

GEORGE C. KENNEY

on patrol and send his B-17s aloft so that they would not be surprised on the ground by the assault on Clark Field that he expected at any moment. His precautions backfired when the main Japanese raid failed to reach Luzon until after twelve noon. By then the need to refuel had forced many of Brereton's fighters to return to Clark or a smaller fighter field, Iba. The B-17s had also landed at Clark to be armed with bombs, the decision having finally been made to launch them against the Formosa airfields.

The stage was thus set for "Little Pearl Harbor." As they winged in over Clark, the Japanese pilots could hardly believe their eyes. One squadron of P-40s was on the ground fueling and the two B-17 squadrons were also neatly lined up, wing tip to wing tip. The Japanese attacked Clark in three waves, two of bombers and one of low-level, strafing Zeros that methodically machine-gunned the array of B-17s and P-40s, leaving a trail of detonating and burning aircraft in their wake. The few American fighters that managed to get airborne were overwhelmed by other swarms of Japanese fighters. Virtually unopposed, the strafers raked Clark Field with gunfire for more than an hour.

When they pulled away for Formosa, with a loss of a handful of Zeros, the Japanese had destroyed 16 of the 18 Fortresses, 55 P-40s and 25 to 30 other aircraft. The debacle left Brereton's Far East Air Force with a total of 17 Fortresses of the 19th Bombardment Group, which had been hidden out of harm's way on Mindanao; two Forts that had escaped destruction at Clark; 22 P-40s; 15 obsolete P-35s; and a few equally hopeless Martin B-10s and Douglas B-18s, both superannuated relics of the tight military budgets of the 1930s.

Brereton nevertheless sent his paltry forces to the attack on December 10, after a day of poor flying weather that had grounded most planes. The feats of some of his pilots provided the bewildered Americans back home with their first, and much needed, heroes. The most highly publicized was Captain Colin Kelly, who set off from Clark Field, his B-17 armed with three 600-pound bombs. His orders were to search for a Japanese carrier reported off the northern tip of Luzon. Kelly and his crew did not find it, but they did spot a large ship about five miles off the coast lobbing shells onto the beaches where the Japanese were planning to come ashore. A half dozen smaller warships were moving toward the projected landing areas.

Kelly veered to the north and then, with bombardier Meyer Levin at his station in the plane's nose, turned back to make a run on the large vessel, which he was certain was a battleship. The crew watched the three bombs curve down toward the target. The first splashed into the sea about 50 yards short and the second also exploded in the water but close to the ship's side. The third, however, may have detonated on the ship's after turret. There was a brilliant flash and a sudden gush of smoke from the stern. Soon the Japanese warship was engulfed in smoke, making it impossible to determine the full extent of the damage.

Just then Kelly and his men encountered Japanese fighters, which

In a Japanese painting, bombers and escorts intent on obliterating the B-17 force at Clark Field in the Philippines zero in on targets at midday on December 8, 1941. Eighteen B-17s, on the ground for refueling, "squatted there like sitting ducks," marveled a Japanese pilot.

them in the difficult art of getting the Mitchells into the air after extraordinarily short takeoff runs of only 700 to 750 feet by jerking back on the control column and pulling away in a near-stall climb. Before long, all the pilots were taking off in less than the prescribed distance.

During the second week of training Doolittle returned to Washington to give General Arnold a progress report, into which he slipped the sentence, "I'd like your permission to lead this mission myself." Arnold's answer was no, but then the persuasive Doolittle went into what he later called his "sales pitch." Near exasperation, Arnold seemed to concede—on the stipulation that Doolittle check first with Major General Millard F. Harmon, then the Air Forces' chief of staff.

"I smelled a rat," Doolittle later said. It was clear that by the time he reached Harmon's office, Arnold would have telephoned, telling Harmon to quash the idea. Doolittle raced down the hall in Washington's Munitions Building, then Arnold's headquarters, and arrived at Harmon's desk before Arnold had had a chance to call. He told Harmon that he hoped to lead the Tokyo mission and—this was not quite a fib—it would be all right with Arnold if it was all right with Harmon. "Sure, Jimmy, it's all yours," was the nonplused reply.

Doolittle immediately left Harmon's office, pausing outside for a moment upon hearing the phone ring. He dashed off when he overheard Harmon saying something about not being able to "go back on my word." He then hurried back to Eglin Field, fearing that he would soon hear from a disgruntled Hap Arnold, but he never did.

When the training at Eglin was finished, Doolittle and his crews flew to California's Alameda Naval Air Station, where 16 of the B-25s were hoisted onto the flight deck of the new carrier *Hornet* on April 1, 1942. The next morning the *Hornet* set out through the Golden Gate and into the Pacific under the command of an air-minded captain, Marc A. Mitscher, whose announcement over the ship's speakers—"This force is bound for Tokyo!"—was greeted with rousing cheers.

On Monday, April 13, during what turned out to be a rough voyage, the *Hornet* was joined by another carrier, the *Enterprise,* north of Midway Island to form Task Force 16, consisting of two carriers, four cruisers, eight destroyers and two oilers. By April 16, as the force steamed on westward, the B-25s were placed on the *Hornet's* deck in their takeoff positions. Doolittle's plane had only 467 feet of runway, but with the head wind created by the *Hornet's* forward motion, that might prove enough for such a seasoned pilot to make a successful takeoff.

Preparations for the extraordinary launch, scheduled for April 19, were going smoothly until the early morning of the 18th, when all plans went awry. The Japanese had secretly established a picket line of radio-equipped fishing boats to patrol the eastern approaches to the home islands. One of these small craft was spotted by the *Hornet's* lookouts. It was soon evident from Japanese radio traffic monitored on the *Hornet* that the boat's crew had seen Task Force 16 and reported its position to Tokyo. The task force and the B-25s were still 650 miles from Japan

Mass production of a winged armada

President Franklin D. Roosevelt, who recognized America's need for enough modern aircraft to fight a war, went before Congress in May 1940 and called on industry to produce "at least 50,000 planes a year." To achieve that goal, 75,600,000 square feet of factory space would have to be built, and 680,000 workers would have to be hired.

By 1943, American factories had not only met F.D.R.'s estimate but surpassed it by 35,898 planes. This was done in part by adapting to aircraft manufacturing the mass-production methods used by automobile firms.

The manpower needs of the rapidly growing aviation companies forced them to seek new labor pools. Migrant workers, once spurned, were now welcomed at plants such as Lockheed and Douglas in California. And the number of women workers, sometimes called the "Janes who made the planes," grew until they accounted for four out of every 10 workers in the aircraft industry.

A woman assembles a cockpit canopy for a P-38.

Workers at the Lockheed plant in Burbank, California, methodically construct P-38 Lightnings on an outdoor assembly line.

Lockheed mechanics put the finishing touches on three-bladed P-38 propellers.

and 200 miles from the planned launch point, 450 miles east of Tokyo.

Aboard the *Enterprise* the task force's commander, Admiral William F. Halsey Jr., knowing that the Japanese were now aware of his position—and could send planes to bomb his vulnerable flattops were he to sail any closer to Japan—ordered the entire force to swing around. Halsey flashed a signal to the *Hornet:* "Launch planes. To Colonel Doolittle and gallant command, good luck and God bless you."

Doolittle raced down from the *Hornet's* bridge and ordered an extra 50 gallons of fuel put aboard each plane. It would take a great deal of careful, fuel-conserving navigation to cover the extra distance to Japan and then to China. The ship's intercom soon reverberated with the message: "Now hear this. Army pilots, man your planes."

Doolittle slipped into the left, or first pilot's, seat in his B-25's cockpit, checked to see that the other four crewmen—copilot, navigator, bombardier and engineer-gunner—were aboard and then fastened his eye on Navy Lieutenant Edgar G. Osborn, the flight deck officer on the *Hornet's* bow. Osborn would gauge the movement of the carrier in the tossing seas. At precisely 8:20 a.m. on April 18, as the *Hornet* had dipped and was on the rise again, Osborn gave the go-ahead signal. Doolittle opened the throttles and, to the immense relief of the other crews, got his B-25 off the flight deck with 100 feet to spare. The rest of the Mitchells followed, the last becoming airborne one hour after Doolittle had taken off.

Doolittle swept in over Tokyo at 12:30 p.m. after a four-hour flight and dropped his bombs in a factory area. Eight other B-25s added their bombloads to Doolittle's in various industrial sections of the city. One plane, under heavy fighter attack, jettisoned its bombs and, hedgehopping to discourage the interceptors, headed for China. The six other planes bombed targets in cities not far from Tokyo—docks and an oil refinery in Yokohama, an aircraft factory and oil tanks in Nagoya, and a steelworks in Kobe.

In spite of Japanese fighters and antiaircraft fire, none of the 16 Mitchells suffered serious damage; but only one landed intact. This was the B-25 piloted by Captain Edward J. York, who headed for the Soviet Union when he found his fuel was too low for the flight to China. York landed safely at an airfield about 40 miles north of Vladivostok where he and his crew were interned. (They later bribed a Soviet guard and made their way back home.)

Of the remaining 15 B-25s, the crews of 11, finding south central China socked in by heavy cloud and unable to locate the planned landing fields, opted for bailouts. A majority of the men, including Doolittle and his crew, floated down in the vicinity of Chuchow, some 550 miles inland and to the southwest of Shanghai. Of the 55 men who jumped, one died when he landed hard in a mountainous area southeast of Chuchow. One crew, which bailed out near Nanchang, was captured by troops of the Japanese puppet government in the area; the pilot and engineer were later executed by the Japanese and the

A grinning Lieutenant Colonel James Doolittle pins a Japanese medal to a 500-pound bomb marked for delivery over Tokyo on April 18, 1942. Doolittle's high spirits and fearless demeanor inspired his men as they undertook this first carrier-based raid by land-based bombers.

Launched from the aircraft carrier Hornet, Doolittle's B-25 lifts off toward Tokyo with 100 feet of runway to spare. General Henry "Hap" Arnold later called the mission "nearly suicidal" and credited its success to the "technically brilliant" piloting of Doolittle and his men.

other three crew members spent the rest of the War in prison camps.

The other four planes crash-landed. Two of the crews escaped injury, but the others had a hard time of it. Two men died in a crash near Nanchang and the remaining three crew members were captured by the Japanese. Of these, only one survived; the Japanese executed the pilot, and the copilot eventually died in a POW camp. The last plane, the *Ruptured Duck*, attempted to ditch in the water off the China coast and made a hard landing; only one crew member escaped serious injury. He took care of the others until aid came from the local Chinese.

At daylight on the 19th Doolittle, in near despair for the first time in his adventurous career, began trying to round up his scattered crews with the help of the Chinese. He suspected that he had lost all of his planes and was certain he would be court-martialed for his failure. But before he could assemble all the survivors he was ordered by Arnold to fly out of China and make his way to Washington. Instead of a court-martial, Doolittle was given the Medal of Honor and promoted to the rank of brigadier general.

The lift the Doolittle raid gave to American morale, civilian as well as military, was extraordinary. For the Japanese high command in Tokyo it proved a distinct embarrassment. Japan's military leaders, who had sworn no U.S. bombs would fall on Tokyo, had lost face. Moreover, since it had happened once, it could happen again. A worried Admiral

Yamamoto was forced by the alleged "Do Nothing Raid" to make a military decision that would contribute to the final outcome of the Pacific war. He pushed through a plan, Operation *MI,* designed to lure out and destroy the American carriers his Pearl Harbor attack had missed. His anxiety to get at the U.S. flattops, thanks in part to the Doolittle raid, triggered the decisive battle of Midway in June of 1942 during which the Japanese carrier force and not the American was crippled.

When Doolittle completed a round of morale-lifting public appearances, he returned to Washington, where Arnold was determined to put him back to work. It was high time, Arnold knew, to send MacArthur a new air commander, since Brereton had left Australia for India to begin forming the Tenth Air Force for operations in the China-Burma-India theater—and Brereton's successor, Major General George Brett, got along with MacArthur's chief of staff, Richard Sutherland, even worse than Brereton had. So Arnold offered MacArthur General Doolittle, while at the same time including as an alternative the name of Major General George C. Kenney, a pint-sized (five feet, six inches) New Englander who had been a World War I fighter pilot and had remained in the peacetime Air Corps. Rather to Arnold's surprise, MacArthur chose the less celebrated Kenney.

Outspoken, scrappy and, like Doolittle, an engineer as well as a flier, Kenney took on the assignment with total self-confidence, unawed by either the aristocratic MacArthur or his watchdog, Sutherland. Shortly after his arrival in Australia in August 1942, Kenney received a savage

A banner welcomes Lieutenant Colonel James Doolittle—standing at center—and his downed crew in Tien Moo near where their plane crash-landed. Upon news of the Tokyo raid and the men's rescue his Alaskan hometown paper joyously punned, "NOME TOWN BOY MAKES GOOD!"

MacArthur lecture blasting what he considered the Air Force's short-comings. When MacArthur stopped for breath, Kenney stood and spoke his piece. He began by saying that he knew "how to run an air force as well or better than anyone else" and that while many things had been wrong with MacArthur's air show, he intended "to correct them and do a real job." If MacArthur still found reason to complain, he would "be packed up and ready for the orders sending me back home." When Kenney finished, MacArthur walked over and put his arm around Kenney's shoulder. "George," he said, "I think we are going to get along together all right."

Kenney proved to be an aggressive air general—determined, innovative and imaginative. He cut red tape and went vigorously to bat for his weary, undersupplied fliers, whom he called his "kids." When he found a colonel in the supply service "whose passion for paper work effectually stopped the issuing of supplies" and who told Kenney that "it was about time these combat units learned how to do their paper work properly," the bemused general had the colonel shipped to the States on the ground that he was suffering from "overwork and fatigue through tropical service."

Once he had reorganized his newly designated Fifth Air Force, chopping out such deadwood, Kenney planned to systematically attack the Japanese ring menacing Australia. He was most concerned with the airfields on the northern coast of New Guinea that threatened the Allied foothold in the Port Moresby area on New Guinea's southern coast.

Borrowing an aged, patched-together B-17 called the *Swoose,* for the "half swan and half goose" of a current popular song, Kenney began touring his command. Taking a 700-mile flight from a fast-growing U.S. air base near Townsville in Australia to Port Moresby, Kenney soon understood what his bomber crews were up against. After making a similar long flight, the crews would have to refuel at Port Moresby's Seven Mile strip before proceeding over the 12,000-foot-high spine of the Owen Stanley Mountains to find and bomb the Japanese bases at Lae, Salamaua and Buna in northern New Guinea. Seven Mile was protected by only a handful of Australian antiaircraft guns and the American 35th Fighter Group, flying the P-39 Aircobra, which was hopelessly outclassed by the Zeros that escorted the Japanese bombers on their daily raids on the Port Moresby area.

Kenney was not happy with the situation, especially after the Japanese attacked Seven Mile during his visit and, as he later recalled, "laid a string of bombs diagonally across one end of the runway and into the dispersal area where our fighters and a few A-24 dive bombers were parked. A couple of damaged P-39s didn't need any more work done on them, three A-24s were burned up, and a few drums of gasoline were set on fire." Since the Japanese dropped their explosives from 20,000 feet, the 10 P-39s that did take off, having a poor rate of climb, could not reach them.

Kenney returned to Australia determined to do a little moving and shaking. He took the weary 19th Bombardment Group—survivors of the Philippine debacle—off missions so that repairs could be made to the planes and phoned in the requisitions himself, informing Major General Rush B. Lincoln, chief of supply in far-off Melbourne, that if the parts were delayed, "I would demote a lot of people and send them home on the slowest freight boat I could find."

By August, with the planes of the 19th refurbished, Kenney was ready for his first "air show." On August 4 a reconnaissance B-17 took aerial photographs of Rabaul, a huge naval and air base recently established by the Japanese on New Britain Island north of New Guinea. The pictures showed that about 150 Japanese aircraft, mostly bombers, were concentrated at one airfield near Rabaul. Shots of the other major field revealed more than 50 fighters. A second reconnaissance mission, flown on August 6 by a young, fresh-faced pilot named Harl Pease, confirmed the first plane's findings.

This evidence of Japanese air strength at Rabaul worried the U.S. Navy, which had set August 7 as the date for the invasion of Guadalcanal in the Solomons, the first American attempt to capture a strategic Pacific island. Kenney agreed to send a maximum effort of 20 or more B-17s to clean out Rabaul while his medium bombers—a few Martin Marauders and B-25s—continued to hit the New Guinea air bases at Lae, Salamaua and Buna that were also within range of Guadalcanal.

On the morning of August 7, sixteen of the 19th Group's B-17s—all that were in flying condition—took off from Port Moresby in what MacArthur joyfully told Kenney was "the heaviest bomber concentration flown so far in the Pacific." The raid was led by the same Richard H. Carmichael, now a lieutenant colonel and the group's commander, who had led the B-17s toward Oahu eight months before.

For the 19th the raid was another in a long line of harrowing missions. One Fortress crashed during takeoff and two were forced back with faulty engines, leaving 13 to fly on to Rabaul. One of these, piloted by Harl Pease, should not have been there. When Pease and his crew had returned from their reconnaissance flight the previous afternoon, they had landed with a dead engine, which put their plane out of commission for the time being. Pease and his men were so eager to participate in the "big show" that they found another battered B-17, which was listed as "unserviceable for combat" but had four functioning engines, and put it back in flying condition by working on it through the night.

After taking on bombs and extra fuel at Port Moresby, Pease's Fort headed for Rabaul with the rest of the 19th. Twenty-five miles from their target the formation was attacked, according to Kenney, by 20 Japanese fighters. The B-17s nevertheless pushed on, beating off the Zeros with defensive fire from their .50-caliber machine guns. At this point one of the engines on Pease's battered plane went out completely; he feathered its propeller and continued on the mission, dropping his bombs on the target. Another wave of Japanese fighters then attacked, singling out Pease's limping plane for special attention. One fighter pass apparently set aflame an extra fuel tank located in the bomb bay. Pease quickly jettisoned the tank, but the fire had already spread. Burning fiercely, Pease's B-17 fell into the Pacific. It was the only Fort lost in combat on that mission—and Pease, who, Kenney said, "had no business in the show," was the first of his kids to receive the Medal of Honor, albeit posthumously.

Although raids like this took a toll of Japanese planes, they could hardly be described as effective when no more than a dozen bombers were involved. Kenney squawked loudly to Hap Arnold, as he frequently did when he felt his kids were being shortchanged, at times firing off a cable a day to his patient chief. Arnold could not send much help. The global strategy agreed upon by President Roosevelt, Prime Minister Churchill and their chiefs of staff called for the defeat of Hitler's Reich first, Japan second. Arnold was constrained to send a majority of the men and planes being turned out by the flying schools and factories— especially the newly formed heavy bombardment groups whose B-17s and B-24s were needed to pulverize Germany—to Britain. But a few new-minted aircraft made their way westward across the Pacific. A few precious B-17s had arrived in Australia by late 1942 and Kenney eventually had enough of them to assemble a new squadron, the 63rd.

Kenney then "fired" his aide, Major William Benn, and put him in charge of the fresh unit. Benn was what Kenney liked to call "an operator," sharing with his boss an interest in unorthodox tactics. Benn and Kenney agreed that high-altitude bombing of enemy ships was generally unprofitable; from 18,000 feet a small vessel, dodging this way and that, was virtually impossible to hit. Why not try low-level attacks? What evolved was called skip bombing. A plane would fly over the sea at minimum altitude—250 feet or less—and release its bombs, which would skip across the water like stones tossed across the surface of a pond, exploding against the side of an enemy ship. Despite the fact that the B-17 was intended for high-altitude work, Benn soon had his pilots skimming their four-engined aircraft across Port Moresby's harbor, skipping practice bombs into a hulk anchored there.

Another Kenney innovation was the parafrag, a 23-pound fragmentation bomb with a small parachute attached. Kenney had invented this lethal device in the 1920s and knew that some 3,000 were stored in a U.S. warehouse to no purpose. He ordered them shipped to Australia and soon found that he had a use for them. The Japanese usually dispersed their aircraft around their fields in earthen revetments that protected them from conventional bombing and strafing. But, Kenney reasoned, if one of his smaller bombers swooped in very low over these installations and seeded the area with hundreds of floating fragmentation bombs, some were bound to drift into the revetments and tear the Japanese planes to bits. The attacking plane could be safely before the slowly descending parafrags detonated.

Kenney decided he would employ the Douglas A-20 for parafrag bombing and turned over the job of adapting the twin-engined attack

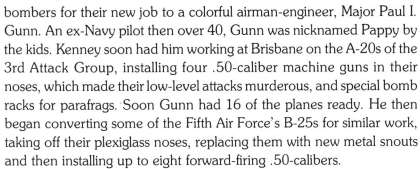

bombers for their new job to a colorful airman-engineer, Major Paul I. Gunn. An ex-Navy pilot then over 40, Gunn was nicknamed Pappy by the kids. Kenney soon had him working at Brisbane on the A-20s of the 3rd Attack Group, installing four .50-caliber machine guns in their noses, which made their low-level attacks murderous, and special bomb racks for parafrags. Soon Gunn had 16 of the planes ready. He then began converting some of the Fifth Air Force's B-25s for similar work, taking off their plexiglass noses, replacing them with new metal snouts and then installing up to eight forward-firing .50-calibers.

Kenney also found a new use for the Air Forces' 100-pound incendiary bomb, which on detonation flung great streamers of white-hot phosphorus over an area about 150 feet in diameter. Dropped on a Japanese airfield, these Kenney cocktails, as they came to be called, were wickedly effective, flaming the enemy planes that the parafrags had missed. The use of Kenney cocktails, parafrags and skip bombing earned Kenney regular denunciations from the Japanese radio announcer called Tokyo Rose whose propaganda broadcasts in English, beamed to Allied forces in the Pacific, deplored his "new and fiendish methods of warfare." But what else could be expected, added Rose, from the leader of "a gang of gangsters from a gangster-ridden country?"

Kenney was quick to grasp the nature of the Pacific war and how strategic air power was to be applied there. "In the Pacific we have a number of islands garrisoned by small forces," he wrote to Arnold in summing up the situation he faced in his new command. "These islands are nothing more or less than aerodromes or aerodrome areas from which modern fire-power is launched.

"The Air Force is the spearhead of the Allied attack in the Southwest Pacific. Its function is to clear the air, wreck the enemy's land installations, destroy his supply system, and give close support to troops advancing on the ground.

Three photographs show bombing techniques developed by General George Kenney. In the first, bombs attached to parachutes float down and explode on a Japanese airstrip in New Guinea. In the second, a Kenney cocktail, a phosphorus-filled incendiary bomb, explodes above a New Britain airfield. In the third picture, a light bomber skips timed explosives across the water toward a Japanese freighter.

"Clearing the air means more than air superiority; it means air control so supreme that the birds have to wear our Air Force insignia." Destroying the enemy supply system, Kenney continued, "means cutting him off the vine so completely and firmly that he not only cannot undertake offensive action but, due to his inability to replenish his means to wage war, he cannot maintain a successful defense."

And that is what Kenney set out to do with his small band of men and their abused aircraft. He sought to cut the Japanese forces in New Guinea "off the vine" by blasting New Guinea-bound cargo vessels and by attacking again their big supply base at Rabaul. He tried to "clear the air" over New Guinea by sowing parafrags and Kenney cocktails on the Japanese airfields. His planes also gave direct support to the small forces of Australian and American infantry under MacArthur's overall command that were clawing their way across the Owen Stanley Mountains and through the jungles on New Guinea's northern coast, slowly and painfully pushing the Japanese from the outposts and strips that most directly threatened Port Moresby and Australia itself.

To help him in these tasks Kenney acquired a pair of new B-17s and in late October of 1942 added 12 B-24s to his arsenal with the arrival of the 90th Bombardment Group. The 19th Group, men and planes, had earned a trip home and Kenney saw to it that they got one.

The arrival of 50 P-38 Lightnings in August and September bolstered his forces still further. The new fighter plane soon proved to be a far more lethal adversary of the Zero than the P-40 or the P-39. This twin-tailed and -engined heavy plane, although not as agile as the Zero, was faster, could outclimb and outdive it, and had plenty of firepower (a 20-millimeter cannon and four .50-caliber machine guns). The P-38 was capable of disintegrating a comparatively flimsy Zero with one short burst of gunfire.

Kenney promised an Air Medal to the first P-38 pilot to bring down an enemy plane. Late in November five Lightnings took off from Port

Moresby to drop bombs on the Japanese airfield at Lae, in support of the Australian and American infantry battling Japanese ground forces in northeastern New Guinea. Each P-38 carried two 500-pound bombs, one under each wing. The fighters climbed over the Owen Stanley range without spotting a single Japanese plane and, once over Lae, flew about seeking their target while radioing insulting challenges in pidgin English to the Japanese.

In time, one incensed Zero pilot began taxiing for a takeoff. Captain Robert Faurot saw the plane and dived to engage it. He was down to 2,000 feet when he remembered he still carried 1,000 pounds of bombs, which would have diminished the P-38's performance. Faurot released the bombs, yanked back on the control column to escape the blast and kicked the rudder to turn and contend with the Zero.

As he watched he saw the Zero lift off the runway, which ran right to the water's edge. Faurot's bombs detonated in the sea and the water engulfed the Zero, which then careened into Huon Gulf a total wreck.

Mechanics modify a B-25 for strafing attacks. Four .50-caliber guns were placed in the nose and a pair on each side to concentrate the plane's firepower in an area five to six feet wide. With such armament George Kenney hoped to gain "air control so supreme that the birds have to wear our Air Force insignia."

A cocky Captain Robert Faurot poses with his decorated Lightning in New Guinea after claiming the first Japanese plane brought down in air combat by a P-38. By December the P-38s' kill rate had greatly widened the American margin of air superiority over the Japanese.

When Faurot claimed his Air Medal, Kenney, who had heard about the curious victory, jokingly told him that, "I want you to shoot them down, not splash water on them."

Kenney, in fact, relished such unorthodox warfare. No better demonstration of the efficacy of Kenney's unconventional tactics would be given than in the Battle of the Bismarck Sea in March 1943. MacArthur's Australian and American ground troops, after several months of costly fighting, had occupied the Buna-Gona area, effectively eliminating the direct Japanese threat to Port Moresby, but the Japanese still tenaciously held the Lae-Salamaua area farther west on New Guinea's Huon Gulf. It was while the Japanese were moving reinforcements there from Rabaul that Kenney's Fifth Air Force gave a spectacular show of its unorthodox weaponry and tactics.

Late in February Kenney received information from Navy intelligence, which had some time before broken the Japanese codes, that a large enemy convoy was shaping up near Rabaul and was scheduled to arrive at Lae in early March under cover of anticipated poor flying weather. The conjecture was that a full division of Japanese ground troops would be brought to Lae to open a new offensive. After the costly victory at Buna, MacArthur's troops were in no condition to battle fresh Japanese infantrymen. The convoy would have to be stopped.

Kenney flew up to Port Moresby, where he conferred with his deputy, Brigadier General Ennis Whitehead, who sent B-24s and B-17s to observe enemy activity around New Britain. Soon the aircraft returned with the news that eight troop transports with the capacity to carry about 7,000 men, and escorted by some eight destroyers (the precise numbers of men and ships are still disputed), had slipped out of Rabaul.

The convoy was spotted again on March 1 when a B-24 reconnaissance flight reported 14 Japanese ships under fighter escort. Another Liberator arrived to relieve the first but lost sight of the convoy as the weather worsened; a formation of B-17s also failed to find the convoy in the murk.

Early the next morning, however, a 90th Group B-24, the *Butcher Boy,* broke through into clear air, counted 14 ships below and radioed the convoy's exact position to Port Moresby. The Japanese ships were then 50 miles north of New Britain's Cape Gloucester in the Bismarck Sea and were clearly headed toward the Vitiaz Strait between New Britain and New Guinea. Now the weather showed signs of clearing up, depriving the Japanese of cover.

While the *Butcher Boy,* hiding inside the edge of a storm, kept an eye on the convoy, B-17s from the 43rd Group left Port Moresby and raced 350 miles to the scene. These eight Fortresses dropped their 1,000-pound bombs across the line of ships and claimed they had left one transport broken in two and sinking and had made two more hits. The next formation, 20 more Forts, found ships burning and dead in the water and then added to the shambles, straddling the Japanese convoy with a close-knit pattern of bombs and hitting two more vessels. A third

A Japanese transport, camouflaged with vegetation to look like an island, is bombed by American forces near Lae in January 1943. Allied aircraft based at Port Moresby were within easy reach of Japanese vessels sailing the Bismarck Sea.

attack left another vessel sinking near the entrance to the Vitiaz Strait.

The climax came the next morning, March 3, as the remaining Japanese ships steamed about 50 miles southeast of Finschhafen. Kenney now had them where he wanted them—within range of his heavily armed skip-bombing B-25 "commerce destroyers" and the A-20 mediums. The weather was excellent.

The attack began with twin-engined Australian Beaufighters diving from 6,000 feet to 500, skirting the destroyers and turning to strafe the antiaircraft gunners on the decks of the transports. The Fortresses came next, raining bombs from medium altitude. Twenty to 30 Japanese fighters of the types the Americans called Zekes (the Zero), Hamps (a clipped-wing Zero) and Oscars (a new Nakajima aircraft) jumped the Fortresses. They, in turn, were jumped by the P-38s of the 39th Squadron. In 25 minutes of fierce fighting the 39th shot down 10 of the Japanese fighters and lost three of their own. Among the American casualties was Captain Faurot, who had achieved his first victory by nearly drowning a Zero.

After the Beaufighters and the Forts had finished their work, a first wave of Mitchells coordinated medium-level bomb runs with more high-altitude attacks by additional B-17s. As the bombs dropped from the Mitchells, a dozen more B-25s broke out of a low cloud formation. These were the special Pappy Gunn B-25C1s of the 90th Squadron with their deadly batteries of eight forward-firing machine guns— not counting two more in the top turret. With these blazing away, the Mitchells bore down on the scattering convoy; some dived to mast height and swept the decks with their fire, while others approached from

Japanese crewmen take cover as a destroyer, breaking from a 22-ship convoy in the Bismarck Sea, is strafed by a B-25.

water level. When they were at just the right distance, they skipped their bombs toward their targets. Squadron leader Major Edward Larner alone knocked a large destroyer onto its side and left a transport aflame. Before the attack was over, a cruiser and a destroyer had been sunk and nine other ships floundered in various stages of damage.

Before the 90th's planes had left the scene, the 89th's A-20 Havocs moved in. The 12 planes formed two Vs of six each, dived from 2,000 feet and approached the remaining ships broadside "at an angle that would have us brushing the masts as we went over," Captain Edward Chudoba recalled. Chudoba sped toward his target, the cargo ship *Taimei Maru,* which loomed larger and larger in his windshield. "I pulled the trigger on the wheel that started my machine guns spurting. I could see tracers and big stuff coming from the ship. I was pulling the bomb switch when a bullet came through the plexiglass canopy. Thirty caliber, I found out later. I couldn't see a man on deck. The gun crews were well hidden. I let my two 500-pound bombs go now, just as I used to release them on calm days to skip against that old wreck at Port Moresby."

As Chudoba's Havoc passed over the vessel, the plane shuddered as if hit. Chudoba was certain he had been struck by antiaircraft fire, but it turned out that he had clipped off the top of the Japanese vessel's radio mast, leaving a dent six inches deep in the front surface of his wing. A small price to pay for the *Taimei Maru,* which sank.

The weather turned sour over the Owen Stanleys in the afternoon, restricting American and Australian air activity. Nevertheless small groups of B-25s and B-17s were sent out to harry the broken Japanese. The crew of a B-17 from the 63rd Squadron scored two direct hits on one ship, setting it afire, then dropped down to water level to strafe the survivors. Later reconnaissance planes continued strafing until night fell. On the morning of March 4 only one destroyer of the original convoy remained afloat. It was soon finished off by Mitchells of the 90th Squadron.

Of the 7,000 or so Japanese troops destined for Lae, only 800 reached port. They were the survivors of a troopship sunk by the first B-17 attacks; of the 1,500 troops aboard, these 800 were picked up by two destroyers, which left the convoy and raced into Lae. By the Japanese Army's own count, another 2,427 troops, whose transports had been blown out from under them, were returned to Rabaul by other destroyers. But more than half of the Lae reinforcements, 3,664 highly trained and fresh Japanese soldiers, were lost in the Battle of the Bismarck Sea. At a cost of 13 air crewmen killed and 12 wounded, Kenney's forces had sunk every transport in the convoy (eight, in all probability) and four destroyers. The Fifth Air Force, with a show of power that startled the Japanese, had canceled out the reinforcement of Lae.

But Kenney was not on hand to hear the final details of the mopping up. On the morning of March 4, when the strafers finished off the last Japanese transport, he left his headquarters in Brisbane for

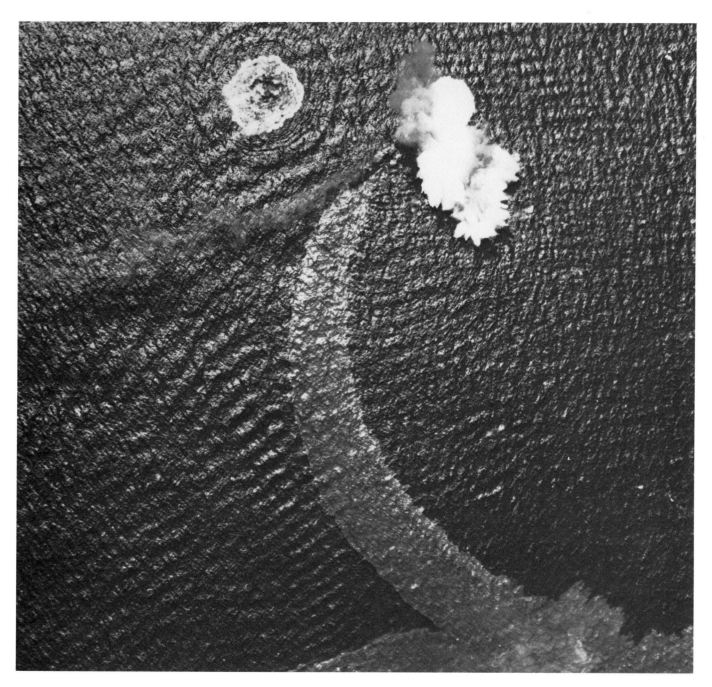

A smoke-obscured Japanese destroyer futilely attempts an evasive turn during the Battle of the Bismarck Sea, leaving a crescent of oil in her wake. The Allies scored a smashing victory, described by General MacArthur as "one of the most complete and annihilating combats of all time."

Washington, well pleased with the triumph of his little air force.

Kenney's plan was to "squawk to Hap Arnold about getting more airplanes"—more fighters for cover and especially more B-17s.

Arnold informed him that he could not have any more Fortresses. Kenney squawked louder until he was told that President Roosevelt himself had stipulated that no more B-17s would be sent to the Pacific.

Why, Kenney demanded to know.

"Eaker wants them," Arnold told him.

This was the onetime endurance flier Ira C. Eaker, now a major general, who was assembling another air force—with a very different objective—half a world away in the fogs and mists of England. 〰

Manning the skies

"Everywhere," recounts the official U.S. Air Force history, "there was breathless haste." While aircraft manufacturers geared up for increased warplane production *(pages 28-29)*, the Army Air Forces—stunned by the fall of Poland to Hitler's 500,000-man Luftwaffe—set out in 1940 to rush unprecedented numbers of pilots, navigators and bombardiers through accelerated flight training programs and into the air. The number of pilots alone who completed training increased from 8,000 in 1941 to almost 300,000 in 1944.

The glamor of the silver wings attracted thousands of eager enlistees. "I've never wanted anything so badly in my life," recalled one former pilot cadet 40 years after his training. Young men, many of whom had never ventured beyond their hometowns or set foot in an airplane, flocked to recruitment centers, vowing—in the words of the Air Force song—to "live in fame or go down in flame."

Only those who passed a rigorous physical examination and intelligence test found themselves en route to a classification center, where they were subjected to further physical and psychological examination. A battery of psychomotor tests, including analyses of hand-eye-foot coordination, identified the recruits as potential pilots, navigators or bombardiers.

Once classified, the cadets were sent on to preflight school to begin their first phase of training. Navigators and bombardiers received their own specialized instruction, while pilots attended ground school. There, to the refrain "Chin down! Chest out! Suck in those guts!" the flying cadets were drilled in the intricacies of military discipline—with daily physical conditioning and examinations in classroom studies ranging, in nine weeks, from simple addition to calculus and physics.

Unceremoniously deposited outside their barracks, a truckload of new cadets arrives at Maxwell Field, Alabama, for classification.

A rookie is fitted with his first article of uniform, a cap. It was an officer's cap, but the insignia on the peak—also shown at left above—identified him as a cadet.

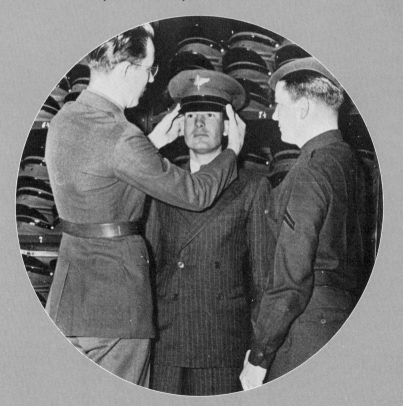

Recruits at Randolph Field, Texas, participate in rigorous calisthenics as part of their daily routine during preflight training.

An instructor watches warily as a cadet lifts off in a Stearman PT-17 on his first solo flight after eight hours of dual instruction.

Separating the men from the boys

After preflight training, pilot cadets arrived at primary flying school eager for the feel of the controls. They got it: After about eight hours of instruction they were expected to solo. Those who did not learn quickly enough were soon eliminated. One pilot later concluded that nine out of every 10 cadets who had begun with him had eventually washed out, most of them in primary.

For those who survived, more challenges lay ahead in basic flying school. Said one cadet of the heavier, more powerful planes used there, "The cockpit of a BT-13 looks like the Grand Canyon full of alarm clocks." But after 70 hours of formation flying, night landings and simulated instrument flying, the men were ready for fighters and bombers.

In a meteorology class at Maxwell Field, Alabama, cadets in basic training learn how to read weather charts.

Cadets hold model trainers aloft to
illustrate precise spin positions as the
instructor demonstrates with a pointer.

The student pilot of a North American
BT-14 receives last-minute instruction while
waiting in line for night flying practice.

Aiming for silver wings

"Where the pig iron is taken and molded into the finished product," is the way a 1943 AAF publication described advanced flying school. The cadet assigned to fly single-engined fighters logged 70 hours in an advanced trainer, mastering aerial gunnery and combat aerobatics. Bomber pilot cadets flew multiengined aircraft, with emphasis placed on formation and instrument flying.

After nine weeks of advanced training the cadet received his silver wings, but his training was far from over. The newly graduated pilot reported for a two-month transition phase that would, a training manual promised, make the fighter or bomber he would fly in combat seem "as familiar to him as his family's front porch."

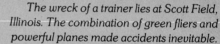

Practicing for night flying, a blindfolded cadet demonstrates his knowledge of instrument and control locations in an AT-6A trainer.

A cadet in an AT-6A makes a run on a towed sleeve target. Gunnery training often began on the ground with skeet shooting.

The wreck of a trainer lies at Scott Field, Illinois. The combination of green fliers and powerful planes made accidents inevitable.

Curtiss AT-9s flown by cadets bank in close formation. Such training fostered air teamwork, a necessity in combat.

An instructor explains the complex instrument panel of a twin-engined trainer to two cadets in advanced pilot training.

"The Three Musketeers of the Air"

While pilots were undergoing specialized training, navigators and bombardiers attended schools of their own. A fledgling bombardier—singled out during classification for his manual dexterity and sense of timing—trained by dropping practice bombs from 500 to 15,000 feet under all kinds of conditions.

A navigator candidate was required, in 100 flying hours, to master pilotage, or landmark flying; dead reckoning, or flying by calculation; celestial navigation; and radio bearing. His goal, even during training, was to bring his plane within five miles of his objective and three and a half minutes of estimated arrival time at the end of a 500-mile flight.

Once they received their silver wings, the navigators and bombardiers joined the newly graduated pilots in operational training units. There "the Three Musketeers of the Air," as the AAF called them, were assigned to combat crews and given further instruction in their specialties before being sent to bomber squadrons.

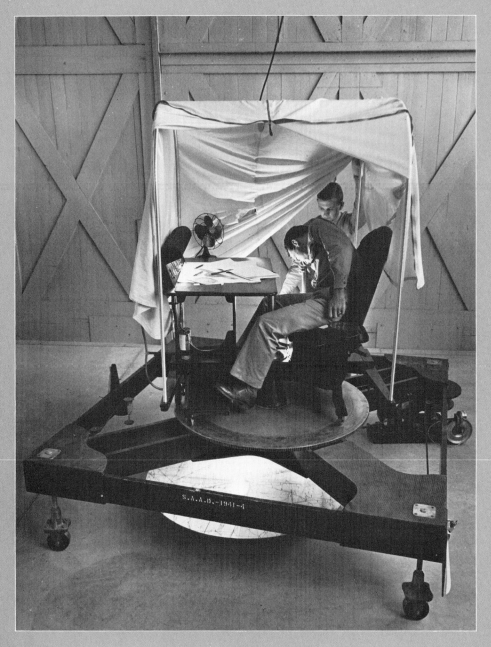

A cadet studying dead reckoning peers at a map through a Navitrainer, a machine that simulated the effects of wind on a flight path.

Students in celestial navigation learn to operate sextants, relating sun or stars to position points on the earth.

Twelve feet off the ground in "high chairs," student bombardiers train bombsights on a movable electric target.

A bombardier cadet in an AT-11 scores a direct hit. Practice bombs were loaded with black powder for easy sighting.

A newly commissioned officer has his silver wings pinned on by his sweetheart. By mid-1945, more than 853,000 pilots, navigators and bombardiers had received their wings.

2

Target Europe

The task facing Ira Eaker when he arrived in England on February 20, 1942, was arguably the toughest undertaken by any of America's air generals. He had been ordered by Hap Arnold to prepare the way for the arrival in Britain of the Eighth Air Force, which would become the largest of all the United States combat air forces sent overseas during the War. He was then to personally forge the Eighth's bomber groups—designated VIII Bomber Command—into a fearsome weapon capable of hammering Germany relentlessly with high explosives. Further, this assault was to be carried on by day—for greater bombing accuracy—despite the fact that the German Luftwaffe's fierce antiaircraft fire and swarming, cannon-firing fighters had already forced Britain's Royal Air Force to give up daylight missions and bomb only by night. And Eaker was to do all this fast— within a year, if possible.

Yet when Eaker reached England that February he had no planes, no crews, no airfields, no repair shops—nothing. America, which had entered the War some two months before, was still woefully short of aircraft, trained crews and everything else needed to prosecute an air offensive, and not a scrap of what little the Army Air Forces did have had as yet been shipped to Britain.

Eaker quietly went to work. A courtly, soft-spoken officer who had earned a law degree in his spare time before the War, he was a model of diplomacy and got a maximum of cooperation from the RAF. His first imposing job was to acquire or construct enough airfields to accommodate a projected force of 3,500 bombers and fighters. Eaker estimated he would need no less than 127. Shoehorning that many—with their runways, dispersal areas, control towers, barracks and mess halls—into a nation smaller than Alabama and already crowded with airfields and buzzing with air traffic presented problem enough in itself. Although busy building up his own bomber force for night raids on Germany, Air Marshal Sir Arthur Harris helped Eaker obtain several RAF fields and suitable land on which to build more, mostly in East Anglia. This coastal bulge north of London would give Eaker's bombers a short air route to German-occupied Europe—it was only 100 miles to the Dutch coast, for example—and to Germany itself.

Construction of the initial fields, however, took time. Eaker could not call on the U.S. Army Engineers—they had yet to reach England—and the British themselves, with so many men in the armed services, suf-

A formation of Eighth Air Force Flying Fortresses makes an August 1943 daytime strike on the Amiens-Glisy Airdrome, a German fighter base in northern France. This and many other similar attacks were designed to cripple the Luftwaffe's forward line of defense against RAF and AAF raids into Germany.

fered from a labor shortage. England's chronically wet weather tended to paralyze progress. As one frustrated civilian engineer complained, "Where there's construction, there's mud; where there's war, there's mud; where there's construction *and* war, there's just plain hell."

Despite these difficulties, Eaker was able, when his machines and men began arriving in July 1942, to provide runways for the planes and living quarters for the air and ground crews. Between the Eighth Air Force and the RAF's fast-expanding Bomber Command, Britain eventually was converted into a vast, stationary aircraft carrier. Eaker also managed to set up such necessary services as a meteorological office—to "study this beastly weather," as Eaker put it—and an intelligence branch whose main job was to pinpoint Germany's most vital industrial plants. With RAF help he also got under way the heavy repair facilities that would be needed when the big bombers came back from missions with engines shot to pieces and gaping holes in their aluminum skins.

Getting his planes in place was no easy job. The big B-17s and B-24s had sufficient range to fly the 2,119 miles from the airfield at Gander in Newfoundland to Prestwick in Scotland, but the North Atlantic's weather—unpredictable in summer and wretched the rest of the year—made the long hop hazardous. To make it safer for the bombers, Brigadier General Harold George, under Arnold's orders, rushed the construction of three emergency stopover fields—two on Greenland and one near Reykjavik in Iceland—plus an alternative takeoff point, supplementing Gander, at Goose Bay in Labrador. Britain-bound B-17s or B-24s encountering storms or head winds, or simply the sullen cloud banks that hindered navigation over the North Atlantic, could home in by radio on the fields, land and wait for better weather.

These mid-Atlantic refuges also made it possible for fighters to fly from the United States to Britain; the longest hop, from Reykjavik to Prestwick, was 846 miles, within the range of fighters with extra fuel tanks. In practice, however, few fighters made the trip by air. Even big bombers, each carrying a trained navigator, all too frequently wandered off course—to vanish in the featureless expanse of the Atlantic. For fighter pilots in small, one-man cockpits navigating with only a few instruments, the flight was a gamble. Most fighters therefore went by ship—along with their pilots and all of the Eighth's ground personnel.

General George's fields in Greenland and Iceland were in operational shape by April 1942, but delays held up Eaker's combat units. The first arrived in Britain on May 11, but it was the 15th Bombardment Squadron, a twin-engined attack bomber outfit, and not the sort of heavy four-engined unit that Eaker hoped for. In addition, the 15th Squadron's crews had come by ship, leaving their planes behind to follow on a slow freighter. Finally on July 1—more than four months after Eaker's own arrival in England—a lone B-17E belonging to the 97th Bombardment Group (Heavy) made a smooth landing at Prestwick, causing a clerk at VIII Bomber Command to make the wistful notation in the headquarters' log: "Arrival of aircraft: 1 B-17E. Total: 1." Soon, however, the rest

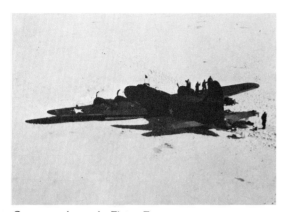

Crew members of a Flying Fortress forced down on a Greenland icecap by a storm while flying their bomber to England wave at their airborne rescuers. After receiving parachuted supplies that included cigarettes and whiskey, the pilot jokingly radioed: "Drop us a couple of blondes and leave us alone."

of the 97th came winging in—minus five B-17s that had gotten lost en route, three crash-landing on a Greenland glacier.

Eaker, impatient to show that the Yanks could contribute to the Allied air effort, did not wait for the entire 97th to congregate before staging his first mission. He chose the only sizable group of trained airmen he had, the members of the 15th Squadron, who, since their arrival in May, had been flying planes borrowed from the RAF's No. 226 Squadron. These were Bostons, the RAF name for a modified version of the Douglas A-20 Havoc—the aircraft that the crews of the American 15th Squadron had been trained to fly. The date Eaker chose for this token first mission was July 4. It included six American crews flying in company with six experienced RAF crews, the dozen planes divided up into four flights of three Havocs each. Their assigned targets were four Luftwaffe airfields in Holland. They were to attack at treetop level.

The mission began to run into trouble over the North Sea, where the Havocs were spotted by German ships, which alerted the antiaircraft guns all along the Dutch coast. One of the three-plane flights eluded the guns simply because its leader, unable to locate the objective, turned around and flew back to England. Another flight managed to slip in and out of its target area, an air base near Haamstede, without loss. The other two flights, however, did not fare so well.

At the Bergen-Alkmaar airfield the attackers ran into a murderous concentration of flak. They managed to bomb through the hail of flying metal but left one of their number burning on the ground. Even worse flak awaited the flight heading for the Luftwaffe field at De Kooy. The Havocs faced a three-mile obstacle course of antiaircraft fire even before reaching their target. The RAF lead plane made it through, dropped its bombs and fled the scene. But of the two U.S.-crewed Havocs that followed, the first took a direct hit and smashed into the ground, while the second, piloted by Captain Charles C. Kegelman, was severely damaged by a direct hit in the right engine.

The explosion wrenched off the propeller and set the engine aflame, forcing Kegelman to jettison his bombs. While smoke and fire streamed from the damaged engine and Kegelman fought to control the plane, his right wing tip struck the ground. As Kegelman pulled back on the control column and the nose lifted with a shudder, he heard the sound of the fuselage dragging along the ground. But the resilient Havoc bounced back into the air and Kegelman nursed his dented plane to its base at Swanton Morley on one engine and a crumpled wing.

Eaker's Independence Day effort could hardly have been called a success: Three Havocs—and nine men—had been lost, and only five of the 12 planes had dropped their bombs anywhere near their targets. Even so, the mission was widely reported in Britain and the United States as an example of Allied unity and American mettle.

Unhappily, Eaker could not follow it up with an all-U.S. mission for a month and a half. By late July, 44 Fortresses of the 97th Group had been ferried by their crews from Presque Isle, Maine, via Newfoundland to Prestwick, and from there to bases in East Anglia. But Eaker soon found that many crews, rushed through training for the overseas move, were woefully unprepared for combat. Some of the group's pilots were inexperienced in formation flying, and virtually all hands lacked training in the use of oxygen, essential at high altitudes. Many gunners, it was found, had never fired their guns from aircraft at moving targets.

Eaker turned the 97th over to Colonel Frank A. Armstrong, an exacting and astute air leader, who put it through an intense training program. The group's most perfidious adversary was the weather, which inflicted its first casualties when a Fortress, lost in the murk over Wales, crashed into a mountaintop, killing the entire 10-man crew.

In early August Armstrong pronounced 24 of the group's crews combat ready—enough to man two squadrons of 12 planes each—and on the night of August 16, eighteen of these crews were alerted for the mission that would be known as VIII Bomber Command, Mission No. 1. It was a modest first effort. Eaker planned no deep penetration of Germany, but rather a short hop across the Channel to Rouen, in northern France, site of the Sotteville railroad marshaling yards. Through these yards, which included a major locomotive repair complex, German troops and supplies were switched to other parts of France and to the Low Countries.

But Mission No. 1, if modest, was highly significant. Eaker's counterpart, Air Marshal Harris of the RAF's Bomber Command, and other RAF top brass were openly skeptical of the AAF's policy of daylight bombing. They simply did not believe that the Eighth Air Force could stage daytime missions without crippling casualties; their Wellington and Blenheim bombers had been ripped apart by the Luftwaffe's Messerschmitt 109 and Focke-Wulf 190 fighters when the British planes had attempted a few daylight raids over the Continent. It would make more sense, Harris had repeatedly told Eaker, if the Eighth would reinforce his Bomber Command by joining in the RAF's night missions.

Eaker insisted that B-17s and B-24s, with their 10 or more .50-caliber machine guns—heavier armament than any British bomber carried—could beat off fighter attacks, especially if they flew in tight formations that concentrated their defensive fire. Further, by bombing in daylight and using the Air Forces' super-secret Norden bombsight—the most accurate mechanism of its type yet invented—the U.S. crews would be able to hit specific targets rather than being forced by darkness to dump their bombloads helter-skelter over the blacked-out cities.

Convinced of his view, Eaker would not budge. Nor would Major General Carl A. "Tooey" Spaatz, who had arrived in England in mid-June to head the entire Eighth Air Force while Eaker continued to command its bombers. Spaatz, Eaker's old friend and flying colleague, was an equally vigorous proponent of daylight precision attacks.

Mission No. 1 was thus a test of the entire AAF approach to air warfare, and it drew a sizable crowd, British and American, to the 97th Group's main field near the East Anglian village of Grafton Underwood.

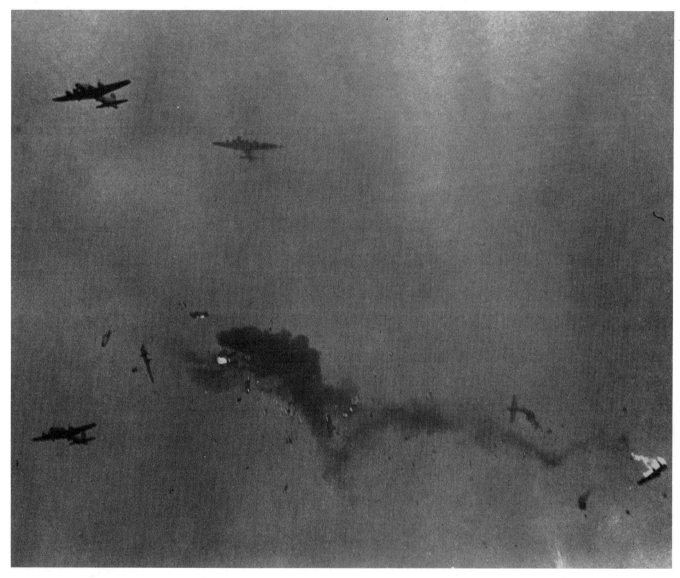

Victims of the weather, two B-17 Flying Fortresses that collided in mid-air fall in pieces through a murky English sky. Such collisions were frequent.

No fewer than 30 reporters from papers on both sides of the Atlantic were crammed into the tiny control tower, and RAF observers abounded. Spaatz underscored the mission's significance by granting Eaker permission to go along on the raid. It was unusual to risk experienced officers with generals' stars on their shoulders over enemy territory.

The mission opened with a feint as six Forts took off from Polebrook, the 97th's satellite base, and broke up into two flights, one apparently pointed toward Dunkirk and the other toward Cherbourg. This ploy, it was hoped, would draw the Luftwaffe fighters away from Rouen. When each of these flights reached a point about 10 miles from the enemy-occupied coast, they were to swerve away and return to Polebrook.

About 15 minutes after these decoys had taken off, the remaining dozen B-17s began lifting from the Grafton Underwood runway. In the lead plane of the first flight was group commander Armstrong. Eaker flew in the second flight's lead aircraft, which was appropriately named *Yankee Doodle.* As the last B-17s disappeared from sight in the afternoon sky, winging toward their rendezvous over the Channel with four squadrons of escorting RAF Spitfires, the spectators began a suspenseful three-hour wait.

Just before 7 p.m. a Fortress was spotted from the Grafton Underwood control tower; anxiously the observers counted the planes that trailed it. All 12 B-17s that had been dispatched to Rouen set down smoothly on the runway to be surrounded by their ground crews, the assorted brass and the reporters. Mission No. 1 had been executed perfectly. The B-17s had bombed from 23,000 feet—above the range of the Rouen flak—and only two had been slightly damaged. They had dumped more than 36,000 pounds of explosives on the sprawling marshaling yard, and later reconnaissance photographs revealed that about half of the bombs had fallen into the target area, damaging the locomotive repair shops, other buildings, rolling stock and rails. The pilots of the few Me 109s and FW 190s that penetrated the Spitfire screen to approach the Fortresses appeared to be rather timid, partly no doubt because they were seeing the B-17 for the first time.

After the first all-American attack on occupied France, a daylight strike on Rouen, officers and reporters watch as the first returning bomber descends for a landing.

Smoking a congratulatory cigar, Brigadier General Ira Eaker, leader of the Rouen raid, answers reporters' questions. "One swallow doesn't make a summer," he cautioned.

German fighters had also kept their distance from the half-dozen decoys, all of which returned to their field at Polebrook unscathed. It was an extraordinarily successful first mission and it strenghtened Eaker's and Spaatz's arguments in favor of daylight bombing. Air Marshal Harris graciously acknowledged their success with a telegram that concluded: "Yankee Doodle certainly went to town and can stick another well-deserved feather in his cap." Eaker announced with characteristic circumspection that he was "satisfied with the day's work." But he knew full well that this raid by only a dozen planes, like his July 4 Anglo-American exercise, was little more than a token effort.

The enthusiasm and confidence created by the Rouen raid among Eaker's crews carried over into the next eight missions, flown between August 19 and September 5, during which not a single bomber was lost. But again all targets were close by in France or the Netherlands and the missions were well escorted by Spitfires, which seemed to keep the German fighters at a respectful distance.

The Luftwaffe pilots were not, however, as reticent as some bomber crewmen came to believe. They were simply studying the B-17, looking for its weaknesses, seeking the best angles of attack. On September 6 the Luftwaffe demonstrated the fruits of this study.

By then Eaker could dispatch three groups on raids: the veteran 97th, the 301st and the just-arrived 92nd. On September 6, forty-one Fortresses of the 92nd and 97th set out for Avions Potez, an aircraft factory at Méaulte in northern France that the Germans were using as a repair depot for their planes. This force came under furious attack as soon as it reached the French coast. Slashing through the Spitfire cover, the German fighters, most of them FW 190s of a crack fighter group, Jagdgeschwader 26, concentrated on the bombers, shooting down two Forts and inflicting the Eighth's first losses.

Thirty-six men show the manpower needed to service and fly a B-17E Flying Fortress in 1942. Later, one more gunner was added to the crew.

Propellers

Mechanics

After the raid on Avions Potez, the wet English autumn weather virtually halted missions for a month—although some more bombers and crews managed to settle in on Eaker's hastily constructed fields. By October 9 Eaker was ready for his first 100-bomber strike, the target an industrial complex of steelworks and locomotive shops at Lille in northern France. Drawing upon the resources of four groups of B-17s and one of B-24s, Eaker dispatched 108 heavy bombers to Lille in perfect flying weather. Because their objective lay within fighter range, they could be shepherded by 156 Allied fighters, both RAF Spitfires and the P-38s of the newly activated 1st Fighter Group of the AAF.

The mission nevertheless suffered ill fortune right from the start. Various mechanical problems forced 19 Fortresses to abort and return to England; 10 out of 24 Liberators also turned back. The remaining 79 bombers pressed on—and were met by an estimated force of 60 FW 190s that screamed down through the Allied fighter screen to attack the Forts and Liberators. Most of the German planes, using a new tactic, came in from the "six o'clock" position (from the rear) and low. This kept them out of the sights of the waist gunners and the flight engineers in their top turrets. Only the gunners in the belly turrets had a shot, along with the tail gunners huddled in their cramped quarters aft of the rudder.

The resulting melee was fast, furious and deadly. One Liberator and three Fortresses were shot down, and the 75 planes that made it back to England bore many marks of the battle. One ground crew chief, Master Sergeant Charles Chambers, on seeing his plane pull into its hardstand with some 200 Luftwaffe punctures, angrily asked the pilot, "Goddam it, Lieutenant, what the hell have you been doing to my ship?"

The battle over Lille reaffirmed fears long harbored by Eaker and his boss, Spaatz: If the Allied air forces hoped to "dislocate German industry," as Eaker put it, and "remove from the enemy the means for waging successful war," something would have to be done about the Luftwaffe. Both the B-17 and the B-24, despite their defensive armament, had proved vulnerable to determined fighter attack. Escort fighters were the answer, but as yet the Eighth had only four fighter groups and most of their P-38 Lightnings suffered from mechanical problems. Moreover, the P-38s did not have the range to reach into Germany and the RAF's Spitfires, which had been designed as short-range defensive machines, could fly only short hops such as the trip to Lille.

Lacking long-range fighters, Eaker and Spaatz considered other means of striking back at the Luftwaffe. One desperate remedy was to send unescorted bombers deep into Germany to attack the factories where the Focke-Wulfs and Messerschmitts were assembled. But before the two generals could map such a plan they received two pieces of jolting news. The first: The British and American high commands had decided to invade Morocco and Algeria in northwestern Africa, both under control of the Vichy French, and then to capture Tunisia from the Germans and Italians stationed there. The purpose was to drive Axis forces from all of North Africa, securing bases from which to stage a cross-Mediterranean invasion of Sicily and, ultimately, Italy itself. The British-American forces scheduled to land in Algeria and Morocco in November 1942 would of course require air cover. Until then Operation *Torch,* as the African invasion was code-named, would have priority over the Eighth for new planes and crews. Eaker would receive limited reinforcements and might, in fact, lose the best of the few bomber groups he had already assembled in England.

The second installment of frustrating news was an order from the British-American high command instructing Eaker to ignore industrial targets, including the German aircraft factories, and to concentrate instead on the French ports—from Brest in the north to the southerly harbors of St.-Nazaire and Bordeaux—where the Germans had lairs for their submarines. The U-boats had been taking a frightful toll of Allied shipping, and it was hoped that the Eighth could pinpoint some bombs on the pens where the U-boats were repaired and refueled. Destroying these facilities—docks roofed with 12-foot-thick reinforced concrete—would be among the most thankless and dangerous of all the objectives assigned to the Eighth during its first operational year.

Eaker opened the antisubmarine assault on October 21, 1942, by sending 90 heavies to Lorient. Escort could be provided only part of the way in and out, for Lorient lay beyond fighter range. Although the weather in England cooperated for the first time in weeks—11 missions had been scrubbed since the big Lille battle—the Forts and Liberators found heavy cloud over the Atlantic. Three of the group leaders decided to call it a mission; all of the Liberators and 51 Fortresses aborted and returned to England.

That left only the 15 Forts of the most experienced group, the 97th, adrift and searching for a hole in the clouds. At the assigned bombing altitude, 22,000 feet, the target was completely obscured. The small

A gunner squeezes into the B-17's least comfortable — and loneliest — berth, the Sperry ball turret on the bomber's belly. The crewman, who lay on his back in the Plexiglas bubble, operated two .50-caliber machine guns with hand and foot pedals.

formation descended under the overcast to some 17,500 feet. Fortunately for the 97th, Lorient's flak crews were caught napping and the B-17s dropped 30 one-ton bombs on the submarine pens. Although five of these potent missiles made direct hits, "they bounced off those massive concrete U-boat shelters like ping-pong balls," as one navigator remembered. But three nearby workshops and two floating docks were destroyed, and two submarines were damaged.

Before the Forts could get away, they came under the fire of 36 FW 190s of Jagdgeschwader 2, another crack Luftwaffe unit. As at Lille, the German planes swept in from six o'clock, attacking the rear of the formation. Two Forts that had been lagging behind were cut out quickly and a third, its wing streaming flame, soon followed.

Although the raid had cost the Eighth one fifth of the attacking aircraft, Eaker followed his orders to continue the assault on the pens. On November 9, a mixed force of 43 B-17s and B-24s hit the U-boat installation at St.-Nazaire. The mission was experimental: The two groups of B-17s were to bomb from unusually low altitudes because of the accuracy achieved by the 97th in its assault on Lorient. The Forts flew into a concentration of some 75 antiaircraft guns that earned St.-Nazaire the epithet "Flak City." Some 50 of the guns were the German 88-millimeter cannon that sent up 20-pound explosive shells with frightful precision. Of the 31 Forts that reached St.-Nazaire, only six flew through the barrage unscathed and three were shot down. The pilot of one of the damaged planes, Lieutenant Charles Cliburn, who was on his second combat mission, reported afterward that a direct hit "knocked out two engines, wounded both the waist gunners. Doggone near blew us in two. We crash-landed in the south of England. Couldn't fly home for a week. Took that long to patch her up."

Two weeks later, on November 23, the Eighth returned to St.-Nazaire on the fifth mission of the thankless antisubmarine campaign. This time the Luftwaffe sprang another unpleasant surprise, the fighters lining up to attack the Forts from an unexpected direction: head on. The intercepting Focke-Wulfs—30 planes from the elite Jagdgeschwader 2—were led by Lieutenant Colonel Egon Mayer, one of Germany's top aerial tacticians. Mayer had studied the B-17 during previous raids and had concluded that its true weak spot was in front. Most of the Forts had only two .30-caliber machine guns mounted in swivel sockets just aft of the plexiglass nose. The .30-calibers—eventually replaced by more powerful twin .50s in a "chin" turret—were popguns in the high-speed air war of 1942; their fields of fire were limited as well.

Mayer had also observed that the top turret's twin .50s could not be depressed to fire on a fighter attacking from dead ahead. It took a skilled fighter pilot to execute such a pass and dive away before ramming the bomber; the combined (or closing) speed of the two planes approached 600 miles an hour. But only a couple of well-aimed explosive shells from a fighter's cannon were enough to flame one or more of a Fort's radial engines or to ignite a fuel tank. And the risky tactic, Mayer rea-

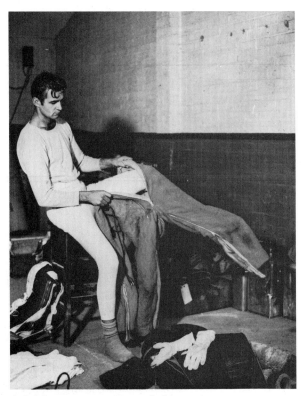

As his first step in getting ready for a
bombing mission, gunner Frank Lusic dons
a heated suit, complete with wire and plug.

Outside, surrounded by the rest of his
gear, Lusic wraps a thick towel around his
neck to keep out the cold during flight.

After slipping into a fleece-lined flight suit,
Lusic puts on a pair of silk gloves over which
he will wear leather ones.

Draped with live ammunition, Lusic
stands ready to board his Flying Fortress. In
his hands he holds his oxygen mask.

soned, was bound to unsettle the B-17 crew members facing forward—pilot, copilot, navigator and bombardier—as they saw Focke-Wulfs, guns twinkling, boring in at them. The effect, he hoped, would be to disrupt the formations and their bombing accuracy.

The principal victim of Mayer's new technique during the November 23 raid was the 91st Group, which had been able to put up only an understrength formation of five aircraft. Of those, two were taken out immediately by the unnerving frontal assaults and two were so severely damaged that they barely made it back to England, where one crash-landed, killing three of the crew. Only the veteran of the previous St.-Nazaire raid, pilot Charles Cliburn, somehow got his plane, *Quitchurbitchin,* back to its home base at Bassingbourn. Cliburn did it despite the fact that he was "painfully wounded," as his Distinguished Flying Cross citation later stated, "the plane seriously damaged, the electrical and hydraulic controls shot away, the right elevator disabled."

Eaker's frustration with the costly and ineffective campaign against the U-boat pens was compounded as his best bomber groups vanished southward to support Operation *Torch.* The Eighth's most experienced outfit, the 97th Group, went first, flying off to the recently enlarged airfield at Gibraltar, which would be the main bomber base for the invasion of North Africa. The 301st Group went next, followed by four of the five fighter groups that Eaker had managed to accumulate, plus the 15th Squadron, which had flown the July 4 mission in borrowed Havocs. Eaker was left with a skeletal force—and the few planes he retained were usually grounded by the weather.

He did have reason to hope, however; he had gotten official blessing for his daylight offensive. This word came from the Casablanca Conference, a meeting of Prime Minister Churchill, President Roosevelt and Free French leader Charles de Gaulle that convened in Casablanca in mid-January, two months after the Allied invasion forces had secured Morocco. Eaker flew from England to attend the Conference and there had a chance to make his case directly to Churchill, who had shared the RAF's skepticism about the wisdom of the AAF's plans and had told Roosevelt so. In his soft, Texas-inflected speech, Eaker explained the problems of switching crews trained for daylight raids into night-bombing specialists. Then he caught the Prime Minister's attention with a chance phrase: "If the RAF bombs by night," Eaker said, "and we bomb by day—bombing around the clock—the German defenses will get no rest." Churchill withdrew his objections to the AAF's tactics and shortly after his return to England used Eaker's phrase, "bombing around the clock," in a speech to Parliament. It was the germ of the Combined Bomber Offensive of both day and night raids that soon became official policy and would wreak havoc on Germany in the months ahead.

Eaker returned from Casablanca to Pinetree, his headquarters at High Wycombe, west of London, with a priority list agreed upon by the

Combined Chiefs of Staff. The German sub pens still headed the list, but they were followed by targets more to Eaker's taste: the German aircraft industry, transportation system and oil refineries. He was also to impose "heavy losses on the German day fighter force." Roosevelt, Churchill and their military chiefs had resolved to launch a massive invasion of occupied France from England in the spring of 1944. Should the Luftwaffe remain as vigorous as it plainly was in early 1943, the cross-Channel invasion forces stood a good chance of being slaughtered before reaching Normandy's beaches. It was up to Eaker and the Eighth to defang the Luftwaffe's first line of defense, its fighters.

How the Eighth's bombers were to do this—their defensive guns knocked down all too few Focke-Wulfs and Messerschmitts during the enemy's swift head-on attacks—presented Eaker with an enormous problem. From January until April 1943, he could draw upon a mere six understrength groups of bombers, four of B-17s and two of B-24s, about 100 planes in all. Eaker may have returned to Pinetree in triumph, but he still had many hard months ahead of him.

Despite his shortage of crews and aircraft, Eaker dispatched the

A 26-acre counterfeit town camouflages the roof of a Boeing B-17 factory in Seattle, Washington. Fear of enemy air attack prompted this deception, built with one million board feet of lumber, one and a half million square feet of chicken wire and 555 tons of steel.

Eighth to strike a target inside Germany for the first time less than a week after the Casablanca Conference. Putting together a force of 64 B-17s and 27 B-24s, Eaker sent the Forts to attack the submarine construction yards at Vegesack, near Bremen, and the Liberators to hit Wilhelmshaven. Excitement ran high among the crews, and the groups vied with one another for the honor of being the first to invade German airspace. A keyed-up bombardier in the nose of a B-17 of the 303rd could not wait to actually reach Germany. As his plane turned in over the Dutch coast, he elevated his .30-caliber machine gun and fired a burst eastward, the tracers arching into Hitler's Reich.

Bad weather and faulty navigation frustrated the Liberators, which turned back for England. The B-17s also had their problems. Vegesack, it turned out, was blanketed by clouds, so Colonel Frank Armstrong, Eaker's most trusted air commander, who was leading the mission, elected to strike Wilhelmshaven, which was the Forts' secondary target. The great naval base, nestled on an inlet of the North Sea, was barely visible through a film of cloud and its defenders quickly began to obscure it further with a smoke screen. Only 53 of the original 64 B-17s observed the target long enough to make a run on it and to drop their explosives. Then, dodging flak and fighting off between 50 and 75 German fighters, the raiders raced for home, leaving behind one Fortress. Like the Eighth Air Force's other pioneering missions, the strike at Wilhelmshaven was not particularly effective, but it was an exhilarating first all the same—and it seemed to prove that the American bombers could attack the enemy homeland without severe losses.

Eaker followed it within two weeks with another pioneering raid, the first American attack on the industrial heart of Germany, the Ruhr Valley, which the Americans came to call the Happy Valley in ironic recognition of the heavy flak concentrations and determined Luftwaffe pilots that defended it. The specific target was the Hamm marshaling yards through which the products of German industry were shipped to the east and north. When Hamm was found to be covered by clouds, the raiders bombed another Ruhr city, Emden, instead.

But Hamm's rail yards were an inviting target and on March 4 Eaker sent another striking force to hit them. The weather was again cloudy over northern Germany, convincing the three leading groups that the mission was hopeless. Two wheeled around to seek another, easier target and one set course for England. That left a lone group, the 91st, which had lost contact in the clouds with the other planes, to continue toward Hamm. Leading the 91st, which had been rebuilt with replacement machines and crews since its near annihilation over St.-Nazaire in November, was 22-year-old Major Paul Fishburne. Finding himself alone with only 14 other Forts—and heading toward Germany's best defenses—Fishburne had his moments of doubt. Should he risk all those boys' lives to bomb Hamm? "It was an important target," he later recalled thinking, "but the other groups had apparently gone to attack an alternate. Nothing would be said if I turned back. We went on."

Fishburne and his little formation encountered scant opposition from flak or fighters on the way in and they placed their bombs with remarkable precision on the Hamm marshaling yards. Evidently the Luftwaffe's radar-equipped ground-control stations were busy tracking the other, larger formations of American bombers that were heading for other destinations. But the Luftwaffe fighters quickly recovered from their surprise and fell on Fishburne and his 91st as they retreated from Hamm toward the Dutch coast. Some 50 FW 190s, Me 109s and twin-engined Me 110s harried the 91st for an hour, the single-engined fighters attacking from above, often three at a time. As one gunner put it, "Those fighters came closer than I've ever seen them in the movies. I could almost have shook hands with one of those fellows."

Before Fishburne had reached Holland's North Sea coast, three of his B-17s had been shot down and a damaged fourth fell into the sea. The 11 Fortresses that made it back to Bassingbourn, all damaged, carried one dead crew member and five seriously wounded. Fishburne's determination and leadership won him the Distinguished Flying Cross, and the accuracy of the bombing his little band had achieved gave Eaker another feather for his cap.

Two weeks after this Ruhr attack, the Eighth staged its first truly successful raid on a target inside Germany, returning to Vegesack and its Bremer Vulkan Schiffbau, a submarine-building complex on the Weser River. Of the 103 bombers dispatched, 97 hit their mark with remarkable accuracy. The raiders also found, unhappily, that the Luftwaffe was becoming more determined, 60 fighters pursuing the retreating force of B-17s and B-24s far out over the North Sea. As usual, a majority of the attacks came in from dead ahead. One navigator, recalling such attacks, was astonished by the German pilots' skill, their planes "flashing, turning and exiting in marvelous choreography. The impersonal quality of the menace was eerie. It was as if we were in battle with beautiful birds of prey."

The menace was also real as the fighters' cannon shells exploded through the bombers' skins. A tail gunner, Sergeant Casimer P. Piatek, recorded in his diary immediately after the mission what it was like when enemy cannon fire caught his B-17, named *Miss Bea Haven*. "After we left the target," Piatek wrote, "we were attacked by about 15 or 20 FW 190s and Me 109s. I kept firing at fighters for about 15 minutes and then all of a sudden a 20-millimeter shell burst in back of me in the tail, knocking out our oxygen on the left side of the ship."

The shock evidently sent the Fortress into a dive, from 23,000 feet to about 12,000. "After we were in level flight again," Piatek continued, "I found out my guns were jammed so I started crawling to the waist position. I got to the tail wheel and we went into another dive. I could see Traban and Ryan [the waist gunners] stuck to the top of the ship. After we leveled out again we were about 200 feet above the water.

"I took one look at Ryan and his face was one mass of blood. I thought he was a goner sure as Hell. Then I went to the radio room and

Home on a wing and a prayer

"You wouldn't believe they could stay in the air," marveled Eighth Air Force chief Ira Eaker at all the Flying Fortresses that returned home on little more than a wing and a prayer. But time and again the rugged B-17 proved itself capable of absorbing remarkable damage from flak or the guns of enemy fighters. Many a crew was convinced that it owed its survival to the Boeing plane.

The B-17 shown at bottom right was almost blown apart by a direct hit over a marshaling yard in Debrecen, Hungary; its rudder cables were severed and its elevator controls were damaged. The green first pilot, Lieutenant Guy M. Miller, managed to keep the Fortress aloft. Steering and climbing by varying engine power, Miller made it back across the Adriatic to his base in Italy, landing safely just as an engine began cutting out.

This B-17 was forced out of formation by engine failure and rammed by the plane behind it. It returned to base with half a tail.

This flak-ravaged Flying Fortress of the 91st Bombardment Group made it home with its ball turret and fuselage pierced by fragments of jagged steel.

Awed officers and ground crewmen examine a mutilated B-17 of the 379th Bombardment Group that reached England minus its plexiglass nose.

Cannon fire from a Messerschmitt 262 jet caused severe wing damage to this Fortress of the 390th Bombardment Group.

Nearly cut in two by flak, this plane flew 520 miles to Italy, and made a perfect landing before falling apart.

saw Gentry lying on the floor with damn near half his side blown out. Then I looked at Phillips and he had three 7.9 slugs in his right leg between his ankle and his knee.

"I then looked out the radio hatch and saw about six foot of our horizontal stabilizer missing. The cowling from our No. 2 engine was shot off and knocked the stabilizer off. The pilot couldn't feather No. 2 engine and it kept windmilling all the way home. It vibrated so bad we thought the ship would fall apart."

The threat from the windmilling prop initially convinced *Miss Bea Haven's* pilot, Captain Guy McClung, that the safest course was to ditch the plane in the North Sea. When he learned of the wounded aboard, however, McClung decided to try for England. He barely succeeded, landing the crippled plane on the first available runway—an RAF fighter field. "We hit the soft grass with a perfect landing," Piatek wrote, "in spite of a flat tire, one engine completely out and two others throwing oil all over the place." The wounded were rushed to a hospital and the rest of the crew stayed with the RAF for the night. The next day they returned to their base to find "the fellows just about ready to distribute our clothing among themselves as they had given us up for lost. The Operations Officer wouldn't let us fly the next few missions. He said we needed a rest. Which I admit we did."

Despite crew fatigue and battle losses, the strength of VIII Bomber Command more than doubled in May 1943 from some 125 aircraft to more than 300. Flying schools in the United States had hit their stride, turning out pilots and other air crew at record rates, and Flying Fortresses were rolling off production lines in increasing numbers. When spring brought unusually benign weather to the North Atlantic, five fully trained B-17 groups that had collected at Newfoundland's Gander airfield, waiting for the winter's last storms to end, took off one after another for Prestwick. By mid-May the Eighth could put up 198 Forts and B-24s to attack three targets in Germany and occupied Europe, and on June 11 Eaker could stage a 252-bomber raid that, finding Bremen covered by cloud, attacked the ports of Wilhelmshaven and Cuxhaven.

May brought other good news: Engineers had managed to eliminate the last bugs from the P-47 Thunderbolts already in England. Eaker could now call on three groups of his own fighters for escort missions. Extra fuel tanks gave the P-47s the range to accompany the bombers across the North Sea and into Europe at least as far as Aachen on the Belgian-German border.

Unhappily for Eaker and his crews, the Luftwaffe had begun to reinforce the units guarding the northwestern approaches to Germany with some 300 or so additional FW 190s and Me 109s. The crucial battles for the skies over Europe were about to begin—and they would dwarf the bloody skirmishes that had already cost the Eighth, by the end of May, 188 heavy bombers shot down over the Continent and, at 10 men per plane, 1,880 crew members. This figure did not include the dead and wounded brought back to England in shot-up machines.

Incinerated in what one eyewitness described as a "lake of fire," a portion of Hamburg lies in ruin after the intensive bombing of Blitz Week, July 24-30, 1943.

Eaker inaugurated these aerial battles with the Luftwaffe—which would rage all through the summer of 1943—with a pair of raids on June 13, sixty B-17s bombing U-boat facilities at Kiel and 102 Forts doing the same at Bremen. He then sent a big strike of 235 heavies on June 22 into the Ruhr, hitting a synthetic-rubber manufacturing works at Hüls, while a secondary force of two B-17 groups bombed automotive works in the Belgian city of Antwerp.

Then in late July, after a three-week period of sodden weather, Eaker stepped up both the size and the frequency of the Eighth's attacks. The result was called Blitz Week and it was the first concerted attempt at "around the clock" bombardment in cooperation with the RAF. On the first day, July 24, the Eighth staged what could be called a diversion in force as Eaker sent 309 Forts to targets in Norway: a chemical factory, a smelting plant and submarine installations. But on the next two days the Eighth teamed up with the RAF's Bomber Command, the two taking turns hitting the German port city of Hamburg. The RAF, sending out 791 heavies on the night of July 24-25, started great fires in the city. Two nights later a similar force, dropping a combination of huge two-ton high-explosive bombs and incendiaries, caused a fire storm that reached 1,200° C., incinerating much of the old city and more than 40,000 of its inhabitants. The American daytime bombings by 200 or more aircraft, although aimed at specific targets within Hamburg such as the Blohm und Voss shipyards, added to the conflagration.

The Eighth continued its contributions to Blitz Week with three raids on three successive days. On the 28th Eaker sent 302 heavy bombers into Germany. One group, equipped with extra long-range fuel tanks, bombed a factory producing Focke-Wulf 190s at Oschersleben, only 90 miles southwest of Berlin—the deepest penetration into Germany the Eighth had yet flown. On July 29 the bombers hit the Kiel shipyards and the Heinkel aircraft factory at Warnemünde, and on the 30th the Fieseler plant at Kassel, also deep within Germany, which contributed to the manufacture of the FW 190. By then the six days of ceaseless attacks had taken a severe toll. The bombers had flown far beyond the range of the P-47 escorts, and 88 of them had been shot down. Crews were dead tired, and despite a period of good flying weather, operations halted entirely for two weeks.

Eaker's force had declined even before Blitz Week began, when three of his B-24 groups—the 44th, 93rd and 389th—had flown to North Africa to join the Ninth Air Force, a ragtag collection of planes commanded by General Lewis Brereton that had helped the RAF support the British Eighth Army in its successful 1942 campaign against General Erwin Rommel's feared Afrika Korps. After Rommel's retreat from Libya, the Ninth had set up several airfields in the desert around Benghazi and at these hot, sandy airstrips the 124 B-24s borrowed from the Eighth joined two other groups of B-24s that Brereton already had. The planned target for the five groups was Ploesti in distant Rumania.

Allied economic analysts had long favored a strike on Ploesti, the center of Rumania's oil industry. Petroleum products were a vulnerable part of the German war economy, since Germany itself possessed virtually no oil. If Ploesti's dozen refineries could be taken out, it would force the German war machine to depend on synthetic fuel laboriously extracted from coal. Ploesti was too far from England for the Eighth to strike it directly, but the Ninth Air Force's Benghazi bases were just within range of B-24s carrying extra fuel tanks.

Chief planner for the mission was Colonel Jacob Smart, who conceived the bold idea of attacking the refineries at rooftop level—for greater bombing marksmanship and to take the defenders off guard. Training was thorough as the crews practiced flying their 60,000-pound planes at hedgehopping height for weeks, dropping dummy bombs on a full-scale facsimile of Ploesti traced on Libya's sands. The low-level attack was daring, but it seemed to have a good chance of success.

Unfortunately, the entire scheme was based on faulty information. Allied intelligence units had assured Smart and the other planners that Ploesti's flak batteries were few in number and were manned by Rumanians who, not very enthusiastic about the War, might duck rather than fire at the attacking planes. The real situation was something else. An extraordinarily thorough Luftwaffe officer, Brigadier General Alfred Gerstenberg, had turned Ploesti into a fortress. The refineries were ringed with 88s and with dozens of 20-millimeter and 37-millimeter fast-firing cannon. Heavy machine guns sprouted from factory roofs. Furthermore, these guns were manned not by Rumanians, but by 50,000 well-trained Germans. In addition, Gerstenberg had 69 Luftwaffe fighters at nearby airfields. The German early warning system stretched to Axis-occupied Greece; German defenses everywhere in the Mediterranean and Balkan regions were alerted as soon as the supposedly surprise raid lifted off from Benghazi.

Brereton's 178 Liberators roared down their runways at dawn on Sunday, August 1. One crashed and exploded on takeoff and 10 planes soon aborted, most of them because sand had fouled their engines. More trouble plagued the remaining 167 aircraft on the seven-hour flight to target. *Wingo Wango,* the B-24 carrying the mission's lead navigator, suddenly and inexplicably stood on its tail, flipped over and plunged straight into the Mediterranean. Above Albania, clouds disrupted the formation and split it into two elements that drifted some 60 miles apart. The plan to overwhelm Ploesti's defenses by having all five groups attack almost simultaneously was coming unraveled.

Further misfortune awaited the two leading groups, commanded by Colonels Keith K. Compton and Addison Baker. When this advance element was skimming over Rumania's Wallachian Plain, Compton's lead aircraft misread a checkpoint and, taking a wrong turn, began speeding toward the Rumanian capital of Bucharest rather than Ploesti.

Baker almost immediately perceived the mistake and wheeled the 34 Liberators of his 93rd Group, the "Traveling Circus," to the left and toward the target. But Compton's group did not rectify its error until the B-24s were over the outskirts of Bucharest. Thus the five groups would arrive over Ploesti in three segments, making them more vulnerable to German flak than had they stuck together. And these first groups would approach Ploesti from directions they had not practiced in their desert rehearsals. About everything that could go wrong did—and Ploesti's gunners, given warning that the Americans were flying at treetop level, began fusing their shells for point-blank range.

Baker's group, roaring toward Ploesti at 50 feet, was the first to arrive. Haystacks flew open to reveal cannon and machine guns; other guns roared from specially built flak towers. Baker's lead plane immediately began to burn, but Baker refused to make an emergency landing. Instead he and copilot John L. Jerstad flew their torch straight toward the refineries, leading the other B-24s of the Circus to the attack, until their Liberator exploded in a ball of flame. Both Baker and Jerstad were awarded the Medal of Honor posthumously.

The rest of Baker's group followed their leader into the flak barrage and succeeded in blowing up the better part of one oil installation. As storage tanks exploded the air became a solid sheet of greasy smoke, while the red-hot tops of the detonating tanks spun through the air like flipped coins. More than half the planes in this first wave failed to escape the inferno. Once clear of Ploesti the survivors were attacked by fighters.

The same reception awaited the succeeding groups of B-24s. One of the echelons belonging to Colonel John R. "Killer" Kane's group lost nine of its 16 planes before leaving Ploesti, and Kane's last wave had five out of six shot down. Kane's copilot, Lieutenant Raymond B. Hubbard, recalled that the "fire wrapped us up. I looked out of the side windows and saw the others flying through smoke and flame. It was like flying through hell." Colonel Leon Johnson, leader of the 44th Group, considered it "indescribable to anyone who wasn't there. We flew through sheets of flame, and airplanes were everywhere, some of them on fire and others exploding."

When these later waves of bombers emerged from the chaos, they were set upon by more waves of fighters. Some battered craft, low on fuel because their tanks had been punctured, headed for nearby neutral Turkey, where the crews were interned. Some made it to the Allied-held islands of Sicily, Malta and Cyprus. Others tried to reach Benghazi, failed and fell into the Mediterranean. Only 88 succeeded in returning to base. The total casualties were 53 Liberators and 310 men killed. More crew members would have died had not a number of disabled planes crash-landed on the level grainfields that surrounded Ploesti. The 108 men who survived these crashes, 70 of them wounded, were made prisoners of war. Overall losses to the Ninth Air Force—dead, wounded, captured or interned—came to 579 fliers. Of the planes that limped back to Benghazi, 55 had suffered severe battle damage. The day after the raid only 33 of the 178 Liberators that had been assigned to the mission were fit to fly.

And, although some of the Ploesti refineries were severely damaged, the raid had little lasting effect on Rumanian oil production; some of the damaged equipment was patched together and the undamaged plants simply speeded up production. The surviving men of the 44th, 93rd and 389th Groups were flown back to Britain to join the Eighth Air Force. Their remaining planes stayed in Africa, eventually to be absorbed into the Fifteenth Air Force once it was established in Italy.

While the catastrophic Ploesti adventure was being designed and carried out, General Eaker was planning an ambitious mission of his own. His striking force had now grown to 16 groups of B-17s, giving him the strength to execute a daring double strike deep into Germany, roughly one third of a fleet of 376 bombers hitting a big Messerschmitt plant in Regensburg, and the other two thirds pinpointing the ball-bearing factories in the city of Schweinfurt.

Eighth Air Force intelligence had singled out Schweinfurt as a high-priority target. Should the city's several factories be knocked out, it was thought, Germany would be hard pressed for ball bearings to reduce the friction in the moving parts of its planes, tanks and trucks. With one blow—so the theory went—the Eighth could do irreparable damage to Hitler's war industries. The Regensburg force would roar in over Germany first, closely followed by the Schweinfurt division. With luck the double-barreled effort would overwhelm the Luftwaffe's fighters. The Regensburg groups would further surprise the Luftwaffe by retreating southward over the Alps to land on a couple of the fields recently built in Tunisia to accommodate the bombers that were flying from there to targets in southern Europe. The Regensburg-Schweinfurt effort was scheduled for August 17, the anniversary of the Eighth's Mission No. 1, the 12-plane attack on the Rouen rail yards.

English weather confounded the ingenious plan. The morning of August 17 found East Anglia wrapped in dense fog. The tough commander of the Regensburg force, Colonel Curtis LeMay, chewed his cigar in frustration for an hour and a half after the scheduled dawn departure and then ordered his groups off into the soup. All 147 of his B-17s made it without accident because LeMay—a strict disciplinarian known to his men as Iron Ass—had drilled the crews in his five-group air division for weeks in instrument takeoff.

The fog also disrupted the schedules of the escorting P-47s. Some managed to rendezvous with sections of the Regensburg force, but the only fighters that LeMay saw from his position in the lead formation, as he remarked bitterly afterward, "had black crosses on their wings." Worse, the 230 bombers that Brigadier General Robert Williams was to lead toward Schweinfurt, their crews untrained in instrument takeoffs, did not leave the ground until three and one half hours after their planned takeoff time. The tactical advantage was lost. The German fighters would be able to tackle LeMay's force, then refuel and be back in the air to intercept Williams' division.

A B-24 (top right) speeds away from a wall of smoke and

flame during the first major U.S. raid on the oil refineries at Ploesti, Rumania. "It was so hot," one colonel recalled, "that the hair on my arms was singed."

Only 15 minutes after crossing the Dutch coast, LeMay's rear formations were beset by the first German fighter assaults—and they still had two hours to fly to reach the target. When one fighter squadron dived away toward its airfield to refuel, another swiftly took its place. Some 300 FW 190s and Me 109s used every trick in their repertoire on the B-17s—head-on attacks, vertical attacks from above, bombs fused to explode among the Forts and a new weapon—rockets. The 100th Group, flying in the vulnerable "tail-end Charlie" position suffered the most. Lieutenant Colonel Beirne Lay Jr. remembered that at one point the 100th was jumped by two entire Luftwaffe squadrons. "The fighters queued up like a breadline and let us have it," Lay later wrote. "Each second of time had a cannon shell in it."

Lay saw a nearby B-17, hit by cannon fire, "completely disappear in a brilliant explosion, from which the only remains were four small balls of fire, the fuel tanks, which were quickly consumed as they fell earthward." After an hour of this, Lay was "certain that our group was faced with annihilation. Seven had been shot down, the sky was still mottled with rising fighters and target time still 35 minutes away. I doubt if a man in the group visualized the possibility of our getting much farther without 100 per cent loss."

Despite the ferocity of the fighters' attacks, LeMay's Fortresses pushed on to the target, their numbers already reduced by 17, to make effective bomb runs, damaging every building of the Messerschmitt plant. Then the surviving planes—minus four more shot down after the formations turned south to cross the Alps—headed across the Mediterranean, most of them reaching airfields in Algeria and Tunisia. Lay's 100th Group had suffered worst, but overall losses were staggering. Of the 147 bombers LeMay led from their mist-shrouded English airfields, 24 had been shot down over Germany or lost to various causes during their southward dash. Many that made it to Africa were so badly battle-scarred that they had to be abandoned on desert airstrips, and three more were lost through engine trouble on the flight back to England.

General Williams' Schweinfurt-bound groups, because of their late takeoff, ran into a refueled and rearmed Luftwaffe. The attacks started at the Belgian coast and continued to the target. This time the Luftwaffe concentrated on the lead groups, particularly the ill-fated 91st, with which Williams flew, and the 381st. The crews were taken aback by some of the Luftwaffe tactics. Flying in a 381st Fort, the *Joker,* gunner Tom Murphy was astonished to see German fighters flying through their own flak to get at the bombers. "I had never seen this before. Normally, they wait just outside the barrage until we fly through it. But today they can't wait to get at us. As I watch, a Fortress from the 91st and then one from the 351st fall out of the sky. No parachutes come out of either one."

As the Forts fell one after another, they left a blazing trail on the German countryside 23,000 feet below. A navigator in the 379th Group recalled watching in fascinated horror "the fitful yellow-orange

The crew confidently has its picture taken under the B-24's tail guns before the Lady Be Good's first and last flight.

The saga of an unlucky Lady

Two sections of B-24s from the 376th Bombardment Group left Soluch, Libya, to strike the Italian port of Naples on April 4, 1943. All but one returned: The *Lady Be Good* and its rookie crew had disappeared on their maiden combat flight. An air search over the Mediterranean and the North African coast where the plane was presumed to have gone down failed to turn up any sign of it, and the men were listed as missing.

And missing they remained, until 16 years later, when geologists exploring in the Sahara came upon the downed plane. The discovery set off a search for the crew; their mummified corpses were found scattered in the sand nearly 100 miles from the crash site.

Flying in darkness, pilot William Hatton had overshot his base by more than 400 miles, apparently because of a confused inbound bearing he received from an Allied radio beacon. A diary *(right)* found near the copilot's remains tells the tragic story of how the crew bailed out when the plane's fuel ran low and began a futile search for water in a land the Arabs know as the Desert of Thirst.

Members of a U.S. Army and Air Force investigating team inspect a .50-caliber machine gun in front of the plane's crumpled fuselage.

SUNDAY, APR. 4, 1943

Naples – 28 planes – things pretty well mixed up – got lost returning, out of gas, jumped, landed in desert at 2:00 in morning, no one badly hurt, cant find John, all others present.

MONDAY 5

Start walking N.W., still no John, a few rations, 1/2 canteen of water, 1 cap full per day. Sun fairly warm, good breeze from N.W., nite very cold, no sleep. Rested & walked.

TUESDAY 6

Rested at 11:30, sun very warm, no breeze, spent p.m. in hell, no planes, etc., rested until 5:00 p.m. walked & rested all nite, 15 min. on, 5 off.

WEDNESDAY, APR. 7, 1943

Same routine, everyone getting weak, cant get very far; prayers all the time; again p.m. very warm, hell. Cant sleep. everyone sore from ground.

THURSDAY 8

Hit Sand Dunes, very miserable, good wind but continues to blowing of sand, everyone now very weak, thought Sam & Moore were all done. La Motte eyes are gone, everyone elses eyes are bad. Still going N.W.

FRIDAY 9

Shelly, Rip, Moore seperate & try to go for help, rest of us all very weak, eyes bad, not any travel, still very little water, nites are about 35°, good N. wind, no shelter, 1 parachute left.

SATURDAY, APR. 10, 1943

Still having prayer meetings for help. No signs of anything, a couple of birds; good wind from N. – Really weak now, cant walk, pains all over, _____. Nites very cold. no sleep.

SUNDAY 11

Still waiting for help, still praying. eyes bad, lost all our wgt. aching all over, could make it if we had water; just enough left to put our tongues to, have hope for help very soon, no rest, still same place.

MONDAY 12

No help yet, very cold nite.

The final entries in copilot Robert Toner's diary relate the crew's slow death in a desert baked by daytime temperatures of 130° F.

flares I saw on the ground," each one a flaming B-17. Against the somber, dusk-shrouded, dark green fields below, "the trail of torches seemed unreal," the fires and black smoke "a funeral cortege with black-plumed horses and torches in the night."

Somehow the survivors of the 90-minute battle that completed the inbound flight to Schweinfurt dropped their 500-pounders and incendiaries with considerable accuracy, making a number of hits on one ball-bearing works that put it out of action, at least until efficient German cleanup crews could clear the wreckage and restore production.

The withdrawal from Schweinfurt was less harrowing than the flight in, for 86 Thunderbolts made rendezvous with the retreating formations above Eupen on the German-Belgian border and started shooting down the Luftwaffe fighters. But the mission cost what one pilot bitterly called "36 junk piles of scrap aluminum dipped in the blood of 360 American airmen," and he was not including dozens more dead and wounded aboard the machines reaching England.

One shot-up aircraft that made it back to East Anglia was a B-17 called *El Rauncho*. With a flak burst in the wing interfering with control and two engines dead, its pilot, Randolph Jacobs, brought the plane in fast with its wheels up. "She must have been going 150 miles an hour when the friction of aluminum on concrete began throwing off sparks," wrote the 384th Group's historian, Walter E. Owens. "The plane slid at a terrific pace the full length of the runway, screeching all the way and leaving a shower of sparks behind. At the far end she whirled abruptly about and careened over an antiaircraft emplacement, finally coming to a stop only 25 yards from a parked aircraft." Pilot Jacobs, emerging unscathed, nonchalantly lit a cigar and said, "I guess they didn't want us to get at their nut and bolt factory."

In fact, despite the high cost, the August 17 raid had not done enough harm to halt ball-bearing production and Eaker was urged to try again. For two weeks after this first assault on Schweinfurt, he once more built up his forces, sending out only short raids, under heavy fighter cover, to nearby targets in France. Then Eaker mounted a succession of missions into Germany that culminated with a series of large assaults on three consecutive days. The first, on October 8, began what has been called the critical week in the history of the Eighth Air Force. This 400-bomber attack on Bremen cost 30 aircraft. The next day's mission, the longest the Eighth ever flew, took 51 B-17s to the port of Danzig (today's Gdansk) on the Baltic and a total of 327 Forts and Liberators were sent to attack aircraft factories in occupied Poland and at Anklam, north of Berlin. The cost: 28 more bombers. A raid on the important railway junction at Münster on October 10, a Sunday, cost 30 more aircraft.

Three days of foul weather halted operations, to the enormous relief of the surviving crew members who were numb with fatigue and the strain of facing imminent extinction in one unpleasant form or another for hours at a time—being blown apart, burned to death or trapped in a mortally wounded bomber during its five-mile fall earthward. Then on the morning of Thursday, October 14, the briefing officers announced to the assembled crews on the English airfields that, with clear weather predicted, Mission No. 115 would round out the week. The target again would be Schweinfurt.

This second attack on the ball-bearing factories proved to be a bloody recapitulation of the first. Once the escorting P-47s were forced to turn back by their limited fuel supplies, the Messerschmitts and Focke-Wulfs ripped into the 291 B-17s with unequaled ferocity. "Wherever one looked in the sky there were Germans attacking," a survivor recalled, "and B-17s smoking, burning, spinning down."

The Me 109s and FW 190s lobbed small rockets at the bombers and also swooped in to make their standard slashing head-on attacks. Twin-engined planes borrowed from the night fighter force stood off beyond the range of the Forts' defensive guns and lobbed in large 8-inch rockets that detonated with four times the impact of an 88-millimeter flak shell. Machine-gun fire, one surviving pilot observed, killed a bomber slowly, but rockets often destroyed a Fort in one violent explosion—with a grotesque finality. As this pilot watched, he saw a rocket rip a wing from a nearby B-17. The wing "folds to the rear enveloped in flames and with the propellers still churning. The metal skin is ripped from the fuselage and the crew can be seen sitting in the cockpit with hands still on the controls. Possibly they are dead from shock or unconscious from concussion. The wreckage begins the long fall toward Germany."

The Germans also employed a deadly technique they had perfected over Münster four days before—concentrating on a single group, cutting it out of the main formation and then slicing it to ribbons. This time they singled out the low group, the 305th, which lost 16 of its 18 B-17s before reaching the target. A trail of crashed and burning B-17s again marked the route to Schweinfurt—and the route home. Sixty Fortresses were shot down over the Continent and five more crash-landed in England. Some 130 planes were damaged, 12 beyond repair.

The courage shown on the raid was astonishing. Even badly damaged Forts pressed on to the target; several crews made disciplined bomb runs while their planes were on fire, ignoring the fact that the flames could at any second detonate the bombs they still carried. But obviously courage was not enough. A few more such missions and there would be no VIII Bomber Command left. Even before the first Schweinfurt raid the Eighth had lost 411 heavy bombers. After that disaster the count stood at 471. By the time the last stragglers came home to their fields after the second attack on Schweinfurt, losses stood at 723.

What the Eighth needed were fighters capable of escorting the Forts all the way to their targets and then back to their home bases. The fighters capable of that kind of mission, the weary survivors would soon learn, already existed, the best of them the offspring of a happy wedding of American design, a British engine and a beautifully simple new fuel tank that would provide enough extra range to carry the plane even as far as Berlin, a 1,200-mile round trip. ❧

One woman's mission

For the crew of *Little Bill,* a B-17 of the Twelfth Air Force based in Algeria, January 22, 1943, might have been just another day. They were scheduled to go on "the milk run," as fliers of the Twelfth characterized the routine, almost daily raids they made on Axis targets in North Africa and southern Italy, when word arrived that today's mission would be different. Not only did intelligence promise a juicy target, El Aouina Airport near Tunis, where German transports unloading troops would be dispersed on the field, but a woman was going along. Margaret Bourke-White, the famed *Life* photographer, had been granted permission by Major General James Doolittle, commander of the Twelfth, to participate in the raid.

Dressed in two sets of underwear—including a pair of long johns—a borrowed sweater, a leather flight suit, a scarf, two pairs of woolen socks and fleece-lined boots, Bourke-White *(right)* became the first woman ever to fly with a U.S. combat squadron over enemy territory. Despite the risk involved, she felt "splendid," minding only the intense 38°-below-zero temperature at high altitude. Her fingers went numb as she took photographs while hanging out over the bomb bay, and the moisture in her breath froze in the hose of her oxygen mask, threatening to clog it—a problem she remedied by squeezing the ends of the hose to unblock it. By hooking up to portable oxygen bottles good for three minutes each, she was able to move from one part of the plane to another. She could then shoot some of her pictures with her head and shoulders sticking out of the radio operator's gun hatch, but she found the slip stream so strong that she gave up.

She did most of her picture taking from the waist gunners' windows, rushing from one to the other and bracing herself against the .50-caliber guns, but "it was difficult," she said, "to keep from getting wound up like a barberpole" in all the hoses and wires of the oxygen and interphone systems.

Three and a half hours after starting out, Bourke-White, and the squadron, arrived back at the Algerian base. Her pictures and later reconnaissance showed that the raid had destroyed 12 German planes and left 19 others damaged. After being cleared by intelligence, the photographs ran in *Life* five weeks later.

A B-17 noses east along the cloud-banked African coast as part of the 43-bomber mission Bourke-White accompanied. To fool the Germans, the formation feinted toward the Tunisian city of Bizerte before striking the Tunis airport.

The mission's commanding officer (center, standing) and his aides map out the raid on a gaming table in headquarters, a former casino.

Officers check maps for emergency landing areas.

Armorers "bomb up" a B-17, using a sling to hoist bombs into the plane's racks.

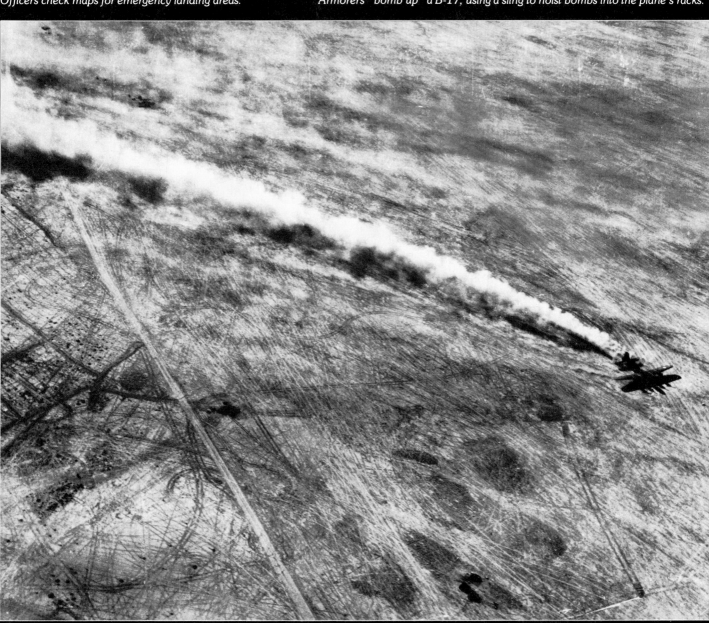

Sand billowing in its wake, a B-17 takes off from a crude desert strip. Only weeks earlier, the planes were flying from muddy fields near the coast.

Mission accomplished, the B-17s head for home as smoke rises from El Aouina. They dropped 90 tons of fragmentation bombs on the target. Viewing

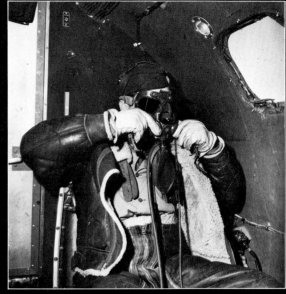

The radioman dons his oxygen mask at 10,000 feet.

Gunners shed their high-altitude gear before landing.

the destruction, the copilot of Bourke-White's plane said, "This is too good to be true."

The tension over, one of the waist gunners lights up.

Back from the raid, the crews share details of their bombing with intelligence officers.

After a debriefing session, the men finally get a chance to eat and swap stories of the strike.

A pilot and a squadron leader, using a knife as a pointer, inspect freshly printed photographs taken by fixed cameras in their bombers.

3

Little Friends to the rescue

During one of the early bomber-escort missions flown by the Eighth Air Force's P-47-equipped fighter groups in the autumn of 1943, a former premedical student from Oil City, Pennsylvania, named Francis "Gabby" Gabreski was leading his "Keyworth Blue" section of the 56th Group over Holland. Ahead of him Gabreski sighted a formation of a dozen Messerschmitt 110s bearing down on a group of B-17s, ready to fire their rockets at the Forts. Despite the agile and deadly Me 109s and Focke-Wulf 190s he could see flying cover above the twin-engined Me 110s, Major Gabreski immediately gunned the 2,000-horsepower engine of his big Thunderbolt and attacked, scattering the 110s before they could fire their rockets. He then jammed his foot on the rudder pedal and turned to dive after one of the retreating planes.

The first bursts from his eight .50-caliber machine guns missed. "I was really wasting ammunition," Gabreski later admitted, but then he "got a real good burst into the cockpit and the engines. All my guns were bearing on the airplane when—about 100 yards away—it exploded and instantly decelerated." There was no way Gabreski could keep his diving Thunderbolt from flying into the exploding wreckage. Burned parts of the Me 110 even came through the vent system into his cockpit.

Gabreski had just pulled up to test the controls of his battered plane when he saw another Me 110 getting into position alongside the B-17s for a rocket launching. Again he pushed the throttle forward and with a few short bursts of his guns sent the fighter burning to the ground. Gabreski then assembled the other Keyworth Blue aircraft, which had been holding off the circling Me 109s and the Focke-Wulfs, and led them back across the English Channel to their base near Halesworth on the East Anglian coast.

After landing his plane, Gabreski found that the right wing's leading edge was dented in several places and that the skin of the left wing was badly torn. The engine cowling was gouged and inside a cracked cylinder an unexploded 20-millimeter German shell nested. Knowing he had had a close call, Gabreski walked into the squadron debriefing and coolly announced, "Two Messerschmitt 110s destroyed and one P-47 half destroyed."

This sort of cocky aggressiveness, combined with superior flying skill, would make Gabreski the top-scoring American ace in Europe, with 28 enemy planes shot from the sky and a couple more destroyed on the

Lieutenant Colonel Francis Gabreski, ace fighter pilot with the Eighth Air Force's 56th Fighter Group, flaunts his 28 kills on the fuselage of his P-47 Thunderbolt.

ground. The same qualities would come to characterize not just the crack 56th Fighter Group but many of the other fighter units that joined the Eighth Air Force in England during the latter half of 1943 and throughout 1944. To the considerable shock of the Luftwaffe's case-hardened veterans, the comparatively green American fighter pilots proved to be pugnacious adversaries. And to everyone's surprise the ungainly-looking P-47, which weighed more than eight tons fully loaded, proved agile enough to do combat with the maneuverable Messerschmitts and Focke-Wulfs that weighed about half as much.

But the build-up of the Eighth's fighter force was almost as slow as the earlier plodding build-up of the Eighth's bomber force. As late as June 1, 1943, General Eaker could call on only three groups of P-47s—fewer than 225 planes—to challenge the 600 fighters that the Luftwaffe had stationed in the West to guard Germany against incursion by Allied bombers. Worse, the Thunderbolts' operational range was severely limited. The heavy planes with their huge fuel-guzzling engines could fly barely 175 miles from their English bases before having to turn back. Thus they could escort bombers only on short missions to nearby targets in France and the Lowlands.

The first technical breakthrough came in July when the 56th Fighter Group's friendly rivals, the 4th and 78th, received several hundred auxiliary fuel tanks hastily dispatched from the States. With these 200-gallon canisters suspended from their bellies, the P-47s could extend their range. When they had used up the additional fuel, they would discard the empty tanks.

The first drop tanks were, however, far from satisfactory. Made of heavy, resinated paper, they had been intended only for ferry work, to enable fighters to fly the Atlantic to England. They leaked so readily that the Air Force technical experts issued warnings against filling them more than half full. Their bulk reduced the Thunderbolts' performance and the 100 gallons they managed to carry would take the P-47s only to the German border. Moreover, the tanks could not be pressurized, which meant that in the rarefied air above 22,000 feet the fuel would not feed into the fighters' engines. This put the Jugs—as the pilots called the big fighters—at a severe disadvantage against German fighters that often lay in wait at 30,000 feet.

Still, the paper drop tanks enabled the Eighth's pioneering fighter groups to give the Luftwaffe its first taste of the trouble to come. During the first drop-tank mission, on July 28, some 50 planes of the 4th Fighter Group rendezvoused over Holland with a formation of B-17s returning from Germany. The P-47s slammed into the 200 or more FW 190s and Me 109s that were assaulting the Forts, taking the German pilots, who did not expect to find Thunderbolts 260 miles from England, completely by surprise. The 4th claimed nine enemy planes shot down, one probable and six damaged against the loss of a single P-47.

Two days later the 4th and 78th Groups sent 107 Thunderbolts on similar missions. The 78th even managed to penetrate a few miles into

U.S. bombers over England in 1943 head toward Germany in the combat-box formation devised by Colonel Curtis E. LeMay for maximum protection against enemy fighters. The arrangement opened up clear fields of fire for the bombers' guns and enabled them to catch the attackers in a coordinated cross fire.

Germany near Haldern, bouncing a force of Focke-Wulfs and Messerschmitts and sending 16 of them spinning down, with a loss of three P-47s. The 4th and 56th, also encountering Luftwaffe fighters, claimed nine German planes destroyed at a cost of four Thunderbolts.

The most impressive early victory for the Eighth's fighters occurred on August 16 when the 4th escorted a wing of B-17s on a mission into France. As Luftwaffe fighters attacked the bombers, the eager pilots of the 4th set upon them and destroyed 18 Me 109s and FW 190s, again losing only a single P-47.

This mission was masterminded by Major Donald Blakeslee, who orbited above the battle in his P-47, directing his men by radio. Blakeslee, who was later promoted to colonel and became commanding officer of the 4th, was probably the most experienced fighter pilot in the

Eighth. He had joined the RAF before the United States entered the War and had flown dozens of missions in Spitfires. When America joined the conflict, Blakeslee changed uniforms—as did a number of his American fellow volunteers, who had also gained combat experience with the RAF's Fighter Command. Blakeslee flew with his veteran group on virtually every mission and finally piled up so many hours in the air (an estimated 1,000) that he was forced to falsify his flight log to avoid being grounded for far exceeding the Air Force's allowable total for fighter pilots of 250 to 300 combat hours.

The 4th Fighter Group's chief rival, the 56th, was commanded by an equally able and demanding officer, a 29-year-old colonel named Hubert "Hub" Zemke, whose instruction manual for his pilots urged them to "scream down with full force" even on superior enemy formations and then "fight like hell" until reinforcements arrived. Zemke and his 56th hit their stride on August 17 when they met, on their beleaguered flight home, the B-17s that had bombed Schweinfurt. Penetrating 15 miles into Germany with drop tanks, the 56th found the bombers being harried by the elite Jagdgeschwader 26. Tearing into the Germans, Zemke's pilots downed 17 planes and lost only one of their own.

The American pilots were able to rack up these astonishing victories with so little loss to themselves partly because the German pilots, when

B-24s form up behind a brightly painted assembly plane over England. Formation assemblies involving hundreds of aircraft were often hectic; to aid the process, battle-weary bombers with identifiable decorations—polka dots, zebra stripes, flashing lights—were used as rallying points. They returned to base as the formations started their mission.

attacked, commonly rolled and then dived away, a tactic that worked well against the light British Spitfire that they were accustomed to meeting. But it was an invitation to disaster against the massive, ruggedly built Thunderbolt, which could outdive all other fighters.

The high kill ratios could also be attributed to the aggressive tactics the pilots had learned from Blakeslee and Zemke—and to the murderously heavy armament of eight .50-caliber machine guns that the Thunderbolts carried. The twin 20-millimeter cannon carried by most of the German single-engined fighters were deadly to lumbering bombers, but their slow rate of fire—about 10 rounds per second—was a distinct disadvantage in swirling fighter combat with 400-mile-per-hour P-47s in which a split second could mean the difference between victory or death. A P-47 pilot, by pressing the trigger on the control column for one second, could snap off more than 100 heavy .50-caliber slugs, some armor-piercing and some incendiary. A single burst could buzz-saw the wing off a German fighter or surgically sever its tail or disintegrate it in a blinding fuel-tank explosion.

For all this, the Jugs were still handicapped by the leaky, clumsy drop tanks, which forced them at the borders of Germany to abandon the bombers to the Luftwaffe's mercies. The solution to this last, desperate problem was the handiwork of one of the War's unsung heroes—Lieutenant Colonel Cass Hough, the deputy director of the Air Technical Section at the Eighth's big Bovingdon repair depot near London.

Hough helped design and test three successful metal tanks. The first, holding more than 100 gallons, began to come off a British production line in September 1943. Another one, which held 85 gallons, was hastily put into production in the United States. Both, being metal, could be pressurized, and Hough's engineering team worked out a system by which pressurized air generated in a fighter's engine could be injected into the tanks. He also adapted a valve developed by the RAF to keep the air pressure in the tanks matched to that of the outside atmosphere. As a result, the fuel fed into the engine smoothly at any altitude. Hough then followed these achievements with an excellent 150-gallon tank.

Hough's innovations had a revolutionary effect on the P-47's performance. The smaller tanks were so efficiently streamlined that they cut the plane's air speed by only 12 to 15 miles an hour. This reduced fuel consumption on the way into enemy territory and thus increased the Thunderbolt's range. The bigger tanks, when they became available, could take the P-47s well into Germany.

The far-reaching benefits of this gain in performance were evident almost immediately. On September 27, Thunderbolts for the first time escorted a bomber force all the way to a German target, Emden, and then home, a 400-mile round trip. On this milestone raid, Blakeslee's 4th Group and the rookie 353rd shepherded one formation of bombers to their target after making rendezvous exactly as planned over the Frisian Islands. The 56th and 78th Groups, which missed their rendez-

out of ammunition, he might have dived again and claimed a third 190 for the day. The German pilot, who had also consumed the last of his ammunition, gave up the chase and left the scene.

Gentile sped for home. He was so depleted physically that, upon setting down at the 4th Group's airfield, he found he did not have the energy to get up; he remained seated in his plane. An intelligence officer climbed onto the wing to question him. "Gentile didn't answer," he reported. He just sat "in the cockpit rolling his eyes and panting."

With the much-admired Gentile safely home, his fellow pilots could find the story of his harrowing experience amusing; one even composed a song, to the tune of "Tramp, Tramp, Tramp, the Boys are Marching," which began, "Help, help, help, I'm being clobbered."

This resilience and mordant humor kept the pilots going under tremendous stress. They were good at what they were doing. They were, in a word, special—and they knew it. This was demonstrated in their casual appearance. Like other air force pilots, most removed the wire stiffeners from their caps, which made the caps as limp as a spaniel's ear. This dashingly casual style in headgear, which implied long and arduous service, was known as the 50-mission crush. The fighter pilots also tended to slouch around with uniform jackets unbuttoned and otherwise evince a rather cavalier approach to the niceties of military courtesy. Their irreverence was typified when, after enduring lectures from assorted brass hats urging the aviators to be "intrepid," one 4th Group pilot, upon his return from a hairy mission, closed his combat report with, "I claim one Me 109 destroyed and a hell of a lot of intrepidity."

While the P-47s, carrying one 85-gallon drop tank, were struggling to fly a few miles into Germany, another fighter, the P-38 Lightning, began to reach England. The air force hoped that this twin-engined aircraft, which had greater built-in range than the 47, would prove an ideal long-distance escort. Equipped with a pair of Colonel Hough's metal tanks, one under each wing, the Lightning could fly almost anywhere over Germany—and several P-38-equipped groups began to do so.

The P-38 soon demonstrated, however, that it was imperfectly suited for the job. On one of the 55th Fighter Group's first escort missions, in November, three of its 48 Lightnings quickly aborted because of mechanical problems. Their Allison engines and high-altitude superchargers malfunctioned in the wintry cold of northern Europe, where the temperature at 25,000 feet could be—70° F.—a climatic condition seldom met in the southwest Pacific, where the P-38 was a success.

The pilots who continued on the mission were soon shivering in the bitter cold—the P-38's cockpit-heating system was also temperamental—and several soon found that their engines were losing power in the frigid air. Over the target, attempting to protect the bombers, the P-38s were speedily engaged by Luftwaffe fighters that knocked down five. Two others were lost to unknown causes, and 16 of those that returned home were heavily damaged by cannon and machine-gun fire. Other

A P-38 Lightning fuels up for a long-range mission. The twin-engined plane, outfitted with two 165-gallon metal drop tanks mounted on wing pylons, accompanied U.S. bombers deep into Germany. Extra fuel in the tanks extended the P-38's escort range by more than 100 miles.

November missions were as bad or worse. By the end of the month the 55th had lost 18 planes over Europe, with four more forced to crash-land on return to England—about one third of the group's strength.

Such severe losses could be attributed to the P-38's shape as well as to its mechanical defects. With its twin engines and twin booms, the Lightning looked like no other fighter in Europe's skies—which meant that Luftwaffe pilots could recognize it even from considerable distances, especially if the engines were producing a pair of the brilliant white trails of condensed vapor, called contrails, that all aircraft engines create at high altitudes under certain atmospheric conditions. Without the advantage of surprise, the P-38s seldom got a jump on the enemy the way the blunt-nosed P-47, which resembled the FW 190, often did. The Eighth Air Force groups flying them were never able to emulate the victory scores of the other fighter groups and had greater losses.

Shortly after the first P-38 groups became operational, a small, sleek and unfamiliar aircraft began to appear at Eighth Air Force fighter bases. This was the P-51 Mustang, which would brilliantly fill the need for a long-distance fighter; it had the range to equal any bomber but none of the P-38's flaws. It proved mechanically dependable, was very fast (440 miles an hour at 30,000 feet), had plenty of firepower with its standard armament of six .50-calibers and could often surprise unwary Luftwaffe formations because it resembled the Me 109. It handled so effortlessly that, as one veteran pilot recalled, "flying it was a sensual pleasure."

The history of the P-51's development began in April 1940 when British purchasing agents in America tried to buy an additional large number of Curtiss P-40D Warhawks to supplement several hundred P-40s already purchased for use by the RAF in North Africa. Curtiss was preoccupied, however, turning out P-40s for the AAF (they were used in Africa and Asia until the P-38 and P-47 made them obsolete). Hearing of the impasse, James H. Kindelberger, president of North American Aviation, countered with an offer to build a better fighter around the same liquid-cooled Allison engine that the P-40 used and to have it ready within the astoundingly short time of six months. The British agreed. The AAF took delivery of a couple of the new aircraft for its own evaluation; they were designated XP-51s.

The Mustang impressed the British more than it did the Americans—by its clean design, extensive protective armor for the pilot, large and leakproof fuel tanks, and good performance at low altitudes. The RAF used the plane initially for reconnaissance missions and cross-Channel hit-and-run sweeps against ground targets. But the plane struck both British and American experts as being un-

Ground crewmen (below, left) carry the six .50-caliber machine guns needed to arm one P-51 Mustang, along with enough ammunition for just one gun. Below, two ground crewmen insert cartridges in the ammunition bay of a P-47 Thunderbolt wing as an armorer services a gun.

fitted for work as a high-altitude fighter—it lacked sufficient power.

Then, sometime in late 1942, an American World War I pilot, Major Thomas Hitchcock, who was on duty as a military attaché in the American embassy in London, learned that the RAF was experimenting with one of its Mustangs, combining the American airframe with the more powerful and efficient Rolls-Royce Merlin 61 engine. Hitchcock urged the Air Force to try the same combination. The result, he believed, would be an excellent high-altitude, long-range fighter.

Despite the fact that Tommy Hitchcock was more famous as a world-class polo player than as an authority on airplane design, Hap Arnold thought Hitchcock's suggested aeronautical crossbreeding might make sense and in November 1942 he gave the go-ahead. The conversion from the Allison to the Rolls-Royce took time and it was not until a year later that the first P-51Bs began arriving in Britain. But with large internal fuel tanks, and fuel consumption about half of that of the P-38 and P-47, the Rolls-Royce-powered Mustang immediately struck the more prescient fighter leaders in England as the plane they had been looking for. Its range was phenomenal: With 108-gallon tanks under each wing, later models of the P-51 could make a 1,700-mile round trip.

One of the first enthusiasts was the 4th Fighter Group's leader, Don Blakeslee, who quickly visited the headquarters of Major General William E. Kepner, boss of VIII Fighter Command, hoping to acquire Mustangs for his group. Kepner was reluctant. He reminded Blakeslee that the Eighth Air Force was in the middle of a huge offensive in which every man was needed and that it normally took weeks for pilots to accustom themselves to a new plane. "General," Blakeslee shot back, "give me those Mustangs and I give you my word—I'll have them in combat in 24 hours. I promise—24 hours." Kepner gave in and some of the first available Mustangs alighted at the 4th Group's Debden field.

Blakeslee's pilots were ecstatic. Those who had flown the light and nimble Spitfire with the RAF had never been enthusiastic about the bulky P-47, rugged as it was. As one member of the 4th put it, the Spitfire was "a sure-footed little filly," the Thunderbolt "a bull-necked, unwieldy stallion." With the P-51, Blakeslee's men had another plane as responsive and highly bred as the Spit. "All ours," Blakeslee told his pilots to appreciative whistles when the planes arrived. He also told them of his promise to be in combat within 24 hours of delivery. "You can learn to fly them," he said, "on the way to the target." Blakeslee was nearly correct. As it turned out, many of the pilots had all of 40 minutes' flying time in their new Mustangs before their first mission.

By the time the Mustangs began to arrive in England, General Eaker's Eighth Air Force had grown to prodigious size. Both new bomber and fighter groups had been pouring in from the States. By December 13, Eaker could send out 637 bombers escorted by some 500 fighters on a three-pronged attack on Bremen, Kiel and Hamburg. It was the sort of force he had been working to build all along: enough B-17s and B-24s to saturate any target and the fighters that were needed to at least reduce the bomber losses. He was sure that he had the tools to execute a New Year's order sent to the Eighth by Hap Arnold: "Destroy the Enemy Air Force wherever you find them, in the air, on the ground and in the factories."

But then, for Eaker, the roof fell in. General Dwight D. Eisenhower, recently named the Supreme Commander of the Allied Expeditionary Force that would make the cross-Channel invasion of Europe in the spring of 1944, wanted his own choice of air generals. Eisenhower had been impressed with the way Major General James Doolittle—the same Jimmy Doolittle who had commanded the famous Tokyo raid in April 1942—had run the Twelfth Air Force that had supported the *Torch* landing in North Africa and the subsequent cross-Mediterranean invasions of Sicily and Italy. Doolittle became chief of the Eighth Air Force, and Tooey Spaatz, who had gone to the Mediterranean to oversee the entire air effort in that theater, was brought back to England to coordinate all U.S. air operations in Europe. Eaker was sent to take over the Mediterranean area. It was "heartbreaking," he wrote Arnold, "to leave just before the climax."

There would be, in fact, several climaxes in the year to come—and more heartbreak. Doolittle inherited a mighty force, but the task he faced was still monumental. Before the Allied invasion could proceed, the Luftwaffe would have to be dealt a shattering blow—and by the beginning of 1944 General Adolf Galland, chief of the Luftwaffe's fighters, had managed, by forming new units and stealing others from the Russian and Mediterranean fronts, to post 1,000 fighters in the West. Doolittle had only four months to batter Galland's force into impotence. To do the job, he set out on a new offensive, code-named *Argument,* that, as Arnold had ordered, would go after the Luftwaffe relentlessly in the air and on the ground.

Doolittle's attempts to prosecute *Argument* in January and February of 1944 were frustrated by the cold and sullen weather. Germany was covered by dismal cloud banks, which sometimes extended to 20,000 and even 30,000 feet, not only hiding targets but also disrupting bomber formations and the planned rendezvous of fighters with the B-17s and B-24s they were assigned to protect. Such misfortunes afflicted the first big mission of the new year, on January 11.

The targets were five aircraft factories in the area of Brunswick, including an important FW 190 assembly plant in the nearby town of Oschersleben. The weather over Germany, which the Eighth's meteorologists predicted would be passable, deteriorated so swiftly as the 663 bombers flew east that Doolittle, told of the worsening conditions via radio, issued a recall order, instructing more than 400 of the planes to return to England. The 139 B-17s continuing on toward Oschersleben bombed through a light overcast and made hits on the city's Focke-Wulf works while another formation of 47 Forts found a hole in the overcast and laid a neat pattern of explosives on an Me 110 parts factory outside Brunswick. But these relatively small forces could hardly inflict

Escorting the bombers to safety

When the Eighth Air Force began sending huge bomber streams deep into Germany in 1944, its fighter command faced the complex problem of providing escort for processions of B-17s and B-24s that sometimes stretched 200 miles as they flew over heavily defended enemy territory. A solution was a massive shuttle of escorting fighters.

Fighters with drop tanks for increased range would fly in relays from scattered fields for successive rendezvous with the bombers. In the actual mission diagramed below, some 200 P-47s were to take the bombers most of the way to the target, three aircraft plants in Germany. About 50 P-51s were to guard them over the target. Some 100 P-38s were then to pick up one leg of the return trip and about 250 fresh P-47s would finish it.

In fact, the mission did not work out that way. Clouds impeded the escorts and 65 U.S. planes fell to the enemy.

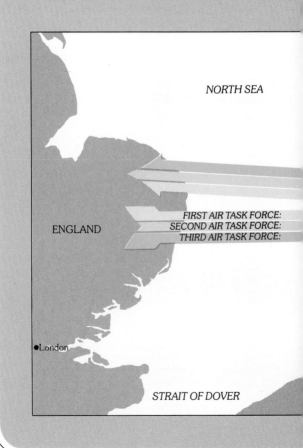

NORTH SEA

FIRST AIR TASK FORCE:
SECOND AIR TASK FORCE:
THIRD AIR TASK FORCE:

ENGLAND

● London

STRAIT OF DOVER

After taking off in pairs, P-47s form up to fly to their bomber rendezvous points.

P-47s fly parallel to B-17s to display their friendly markings to the bombers.

A P-47 chases a Focke-Wulf 190 trying to penetrate the bomber stream's fighter cover.

Their fuel tanks nearly empty, returning P-47s peel off swiftly to land.

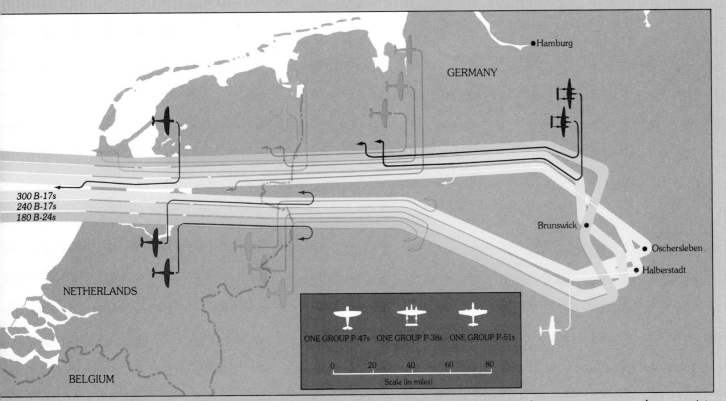

The scheme for a raid on northern Germany shows 14 groups of fighters meeting the three-force bomber stream at seven rendezvous points.

the sort of damage Doolittle had envisioned for his first big effort.

The weather also disrupted the timing of the fighters assigned to guard the bombers in relays, meeting and escorting them during successive stages of the inward and outward flights. As a result, 60 of the big planes went down, the same number that had been lost on the catastrophic second Schweinfurt raid in October. The January 11 raid proved only that when poor weather disrupted the fighter escorts the Luftwaffe could still inflict savage losses. Yet Doolittle and his boss, Tooey Spaatz, had no choice but to mount more missions. With the Normandy invasion still scheduled for May, time was running out.

In late February, Doolittle sent out not just one raid but a series of five big strikes over a period of six days. Big Week, as this massive effort came to be called, began on the morning of Sunday, February 20. The meteorologists promised a high-pressure area moving across central Germany, which would bring several days of clear weather. Three separate air forces—the RAF, the Eighth and the newly reinforced Fifteenth flying from Italy—would combine in a bomber offensive against the aircraft factories supplying the Luftwaffe.

RAF's Bomber Command made its initial contribution by striking at Berlin and Leipzig during the night of February 19. On the next day the Eighth Air Force put up 964 B-24s and B-17s and every fighter group in Britain. The weather was not as fine as predicted; over East Anglia and parts of Germany it was murky and drizzling. Nevertheless, the nearly 1,800 bombers and fighters took off, climbed through the fog and assembled above the various radio beacons, called splashers, that served as electronic signposts. The bombers were to attack a cluster of aircraft plants from Brunswick in the north to Gotha in the south.

But once more weather negated most of this carefully planned, massive effort. Only a quarter of the bombers hit their primary targets with any perceptible effect. On the plus side, the Luftwaffe had also been discomfited by the clouds, which made interception difficult, and only 21 B-17s and 24s went down, a light loss from so huge a mission.

The next day, February 21, poor weather again frustrated both the attackers and defenders. But on the following day, although flying conditions were still poor, Doolittle ordered aloft some 800 bombers. When the 289 B-17s and B-24s that fought through the clouds reached German airspace, furious battles developed around them. It was January 11 over again, except that the fighter escort managed to make several interceptions as the Luftwaffe sliced into the bomber formations. The American fighters claimed 60 enemy planes to 41 bombers shot down.

After an enforced day of rest because of even worse weather, a high-pressure area was promised, and Doolittle sent off more than 800 bombers and 767 fighters on February 24 and slightly fewer than 800 bombers again on February 25 as Big Week reached its climax. Bombs rained down on aircraft-manufacturing plants all over the Reich. In the two days the Eighth lost 80 bombers, but their gunners and the escorting fighters destroyed more than 100 enemy aircraft.

Now the air war over Europe was becoming a bitter battle of attrition, and the Eighth was favored to win it. With fresh bomber groups still arriving to enlarge his force, and with replacement crews and machines reinforcing the chewed-up units, Doolittle could afford his losses. He knew that the Luftwaffe, although evidently still receiving an adequate supply of planes despite repeated bombings of the aircraft factories, was losing its irreplaceable veteran pilots.

The bomber group leaders and their crews were naturally dubious about such a battering-ram strategy—and about being ordered to fly so often in perilous weather. They appreciated Doolittle's intentions even less when he anounced a few days after the conclusion of Big Week that a bomber crew's tour of duty would be stretched from 25 missions to 30—on the ground that "it took about ten missions before a team really became first class." He added that for the crucial 1944 missions the Eighth would need all the experienced crews it could muster.

The bomber men had still less regard for Doolittle after he had visited General Kepner's headquarters at Bushey Hall, northwest of London, in early March. On Kepner's office wall was the motto of VIII Fighter Command: "Our Mission is to Bring the Bombers Back." Doolittle ordered Kepner to take the sign down. "From now on that no longer holds," he said. "Your mission is to destroy the German Air Force." Some fighters would stick to their escort duties as before, but others would be free to leave the bombers and pursue the Luftwaffe, strafing airfields if the enemy fighters refused to come up to do battle.

Kepner was delighted; an attack-minded fighter expert, he was sure his groups, given free rein, could rapidly drive the Luftwaffe from the sky. But among the bomber men the reaction was universally negative. Without the presence of the Little Friends, as bomber crews called the escorting fighters, the Bandits (German fighters) would be back in even greater force to slice their planes to shreds. "It took a long time for the bombers to accept the idea, if they ever really did," Kepner recalled. It was a calculated gamble on Doolittle's part. He had no way of knowing whether his bomber losses would reach intolerable levels before Kepner's fighters could beat down the enemy. Though the gamble ultimately paid off, it remained difficult to convince the bomber crews that Doolittle had not taken inordinate risks with their lives.

He soon took another gamble. This time he deliberately chose a target not for the strategic industries it contained, but rather because it was a city that the German fighter force would be obliged to defend with every available machine—Berlin. Doolittle's purpose was simple: to lure the Luftwaffe into a series of climactic battles, and destroy it.

The first two missions to Big B, as the Eighth's crews called the German capital, ran into the same sort of weather that had plagued Big Week. On March 3, all of the 900 bombers sent out were recalled or directed to other targets because persistent storms blocked the route into northeastern Germany. On March 4 conditions were much the same. The 500 Forts dispatched were again recalled or sent to other targets after they had already flown deep inside the Reich. This time, however, two maverick groups, including the much-battered 100th, plunged on into the storm clouds blocking the route, later claiming that they had not heard the recall order on their radios. They became the first U.S. planes to bomb Berlin—very inaccurately, as it turned out.

On March 6, the Eighth once again set out for Berlin and this time made it, in force. As Doolittle expected, the incursion ignited one of the great air battles of the War. Some 400 Luftwaffe fighters rose to intercept the 660 bombers and 800 fighter escorts as they droned past Osnabrück and Hanover.

Bob Johnson, who was on his way to becoming the Eighth's second-ranking ace, after Gabreski, recalled that he first spotted the German fighters over Dümmer Lake, west of Hanover. Leading an eight-plane flight of the 56th, Johnson ordered an attack on the lead element of 50 Focke-Wulfs, only to find there were 50 more German fighters flying top cover for the lead group, and 50 more covering the left flank.

As Johnson's small flight tore after the Luftwaffe fighters, the Focke-Wulfs turned to fly straight at the leading bomber formation—60 B-17s in the Eighth's standard defensive formation, called a combat box, of squadrons stacked above squadrons that covered a square mile of sky. As the onrushing Germans approached the bombers, they fired rockets, then began raking the Forts with cannon fire. "The 20-millimeter cannon shells exploded with brilliant white flashes," Johnson recalled, while the rockets, "weaving an erratic path" as they neared the bombers, painted "strange flame-and-smoke trails in the sky behind them."

Johnson felt sick with futility, since his eight-plane flight could do little to stop the Germans. Meanwhile the Big Friends—as fighter men called the bombers—began to explode or plummet to earth trailing flame. "Within minutes the churning mass of planes spread over a vast area. The bombers, their ranks thinned and their surviving members badly bruised, crashed onward through milling fighters and angry flak bursts. All around the bombers the Focke-Wulfs had scattered, some to cut down the cripples, the others to evade the Thunderbolts."

Now it was Johnson's turn. Spotting a couple of Messerschmitts attacking a wounded bomber, he pulled his P-47 into a climb. As he gave chase, "the lead Messerschmitt suddenly stopped smoking. It was a complete giveaway; I knew that at this instant he'd cut power. I chopped the throttle to prevent overrunning the enemy fighter. I skidded to my right, half rolled to my left, wings vertical." As Johnson's P-47 whirled around, it sliced inside the arc made by the Me 109 in its wheeling turn. "I saw the pilot look up behind him, gaping, as the Thunderbolt loomed inside of his turn, both wings flaming with all eight guns."

Frantic to escape, the German pilot dived. "Now I had him dead to rights; I closed rapidly as the ground rushed toward our two planes, squeezing out short bursts. White flashes leaped all over the fuselage and wings. I was scoring good hits that were cutting up the Messerschmitt. He didn't give up easily, and racked his fighter around in a

Eighth Air Force bombers and their weaving fighter escorts etch the sky over Germany with white contrails. The telltale streaks, composed of condensed moisture discharged as vapor with the aircraft engine exhaust, usually occurred when high-altitude temperatures dropped below −29° F.

wicked left turn. I got another burst into him; some of the slugs tore into his canopy. The fighter belched forth a thick cloud of smoke," and that was it: Johnson looked back and saw "a flaming mess on the ground."

The epic March 6 air battle, which involved a total of more than 1,800 aircraft, cost the Eighth Air Force dearly. Sixty-nine of the 660 bombers that attacked went down. But the price was high for the Luftwaffe, too. American fighters, some pursuing the German planes right back to their fields, destroyed 81 Focke-Wulfs and Messerschmitts. These kills were followed by more on March 8, when 79 more German fighters were shot down. A week later another massive raid, on aircraft factories near Brunswick, produced 35 more kills. According to Bob Johnson, the March raids "were the knockout, the crisis, the crunch for the Germans." German fighter chief Galland conceded in a report he wrote in April that "the standard of the Americans is extraordinarily high. The day fighters have lost more than 1,000 aircraft during the last four months, among them our best officers. These gaps cannot be filled."

The seriousness of the crisis was not lost on Hermann Göring, head of the Luftwaffe. In an interview after the War, Göring admitted that when American bombers escorted by long-range fighters flew over Berlin in daylight, "I knew the jig was up."   ∿

A pride of American warplanes

"Overwhelming air superiority" was the nation's aviation goal when America entered the War in 1941. To meet it, U.S. industry produced more than 137,000 combat aircraft over the next four years and experimented with hundreds of new designs engineered to outfly and outfight the enemy's best. The finest results of this effort are displayed here and on the following pages. The dates on which each model shown entered service are given in parentheses. Aircraft on adjacent pages are reproduced in scale.

Bombers were the backbone of the air force, and in the four-engined B-17 and B-24 (which is treated separately on pages 130-133) America had two of the most effective strategic bombers in the world. Near the end of the War the larger and better B-29 superseded them both. These giants were augmented by smaller bombers built for lower-altitude attacks and tactical ground support: the B-25 Mitchell bomber, famous as the first U.S. plane to bomb Japan, in 1942; the temperamental Martin B-26, which had better performance than the B-25 but was tricky to fly because of its short wings; and the Douglas A-20 attack bomber, used in large numbers by Britain and the Soviet Union as well as America.

The bomber force was supplemented by a fighter arm that grew in strength throughout the War. The twin-tailed P-38 Lightning was the first U.S. fighter able to hold its own against the Japanese Zero. It was soon joined by the rugged P-47 Thunderbolt and the P-51 Mustang, perhaps the greatest all-around fighter of the War. The three proved equally potent as fighter-bombers when fitted with underwing bombs.

The Northrop P-61 fighter was in a class by itself: Equipped with an advanced nose-mounted radar developed by American scientists, this unconventional plane helped the Allies to win command of the air at night.

NORTH AMERICAN B-25J MITCHELL MEDIUM BOMBER (1943)
Named for air-power advocate General William "Billy" Mitchell, the versatile B-25 served in every theater of the War. Adapted for strafing attacks by the 396th Bomb Squadron in the central Pacific, B-25s such as this one had 12 forward-firing machine guns and carried 3,000 pounds of bombs.

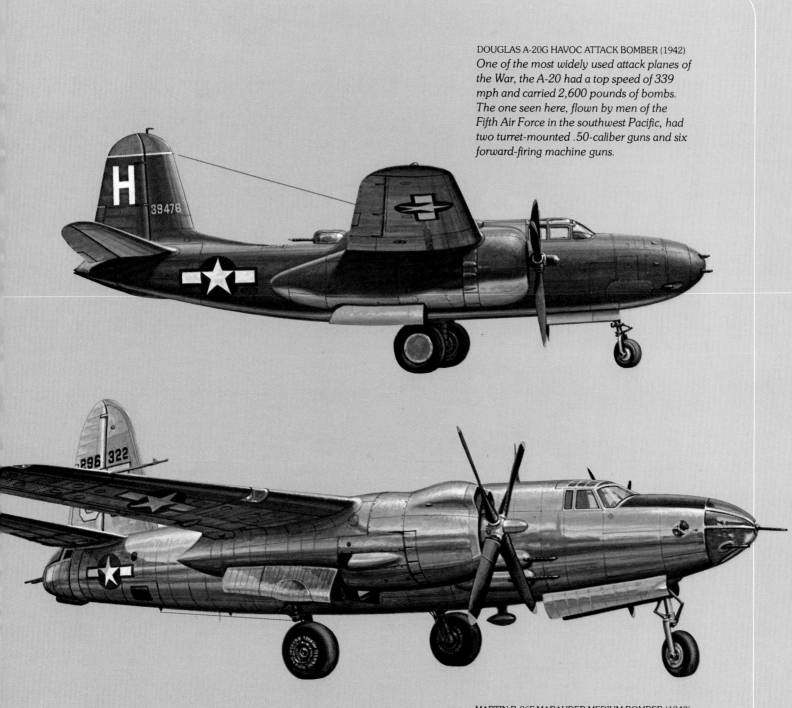

DOUGLAS A-20G HAVOC ATTACK BOMBER (1942)
One of the most widely used attack planes of the War, the A-20 had a top speed of 339 mph and carried 2,600 pounds of bombs. The one seen here, flown by men of the Fifth Air Force in the southwest Pacific, had two turret-mounted .50-caliber guns and six forward-firing machine guns.

MARTIN B-26F MARAUDER MEDIUM BOMBER (1943)
With a top speed of 317 mph the B-26 was extremely fast but required a highly skilled pilot to land it. Armed with 11 machine guns and 4,000 pounds of bombs, it was powered by two 2,000-hp radial engines and had a maximum range of 1,100 miles.

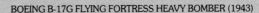

BOEING B-17G FLYING FORTRESS HEAVY BOMBER (1943)
This legendary bomber, whose nickname came from its heavy defensive armament, had a 104-foot wingspan, weighed 65,500 pounds and could carry 17,600 pounds of bombs. The plane shown here—armed with 13 machine guns—flew with the Fifteenth Air Force, based near Foggia, Italy.

BOEING B-29 SUPERFORTRESS (1944)
A 141-foot wingspan and gross weight of 141,000 pounds made the B-29 the largest operational bomber of the War. Used only against the Japanese, it relied on its speed and heavy defensive armament to render it almost invulnerable to enemy fighters. In August 1945 B-29s dropped the first atomic bombs on Hiroshima and Nagasaki.

NORTH AMERICAN P-51D MUSTANG (1944)
Six wing-mounted machine guns, a top speed of 437 mph and unmatched maneuverability made the P-51 a brilliant fighter and one of the most famous planes of the War. More than 15,000 Mustangs were built; this one, ace Charles Yeager's Glamorous Glen III, flew with the Eighth Air Force based in England.

LOCKHEED P-38J LIGHTNING FIGHTER (1943)
*Powered by two 1,425-hp liquid-cooled
engines, the P-38 had a top speed of 414
mph and carried a 20-mm. cannon and four
machine guns in its nose. Designed as a
high-altitude interceptor, the P-38 shot
down more Japanese planes than any other
U.S. fighter; the one shown here served with
the Thirteenth Air Force in the South Pacific.*

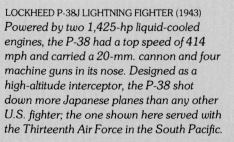

REPUBLIC P-47D THUNDERBOLT (1943)
*Nicknamed the Jug because of its stubby,
rounded fuselage, the P-47 was extremely
nimble. Powered by a 2,300-hp radial
engine, it had a top speed of 428 mph and
carried eight wing-mounted machine guns;
this particular plane was based with the
394th Fighter Squadron in France.*

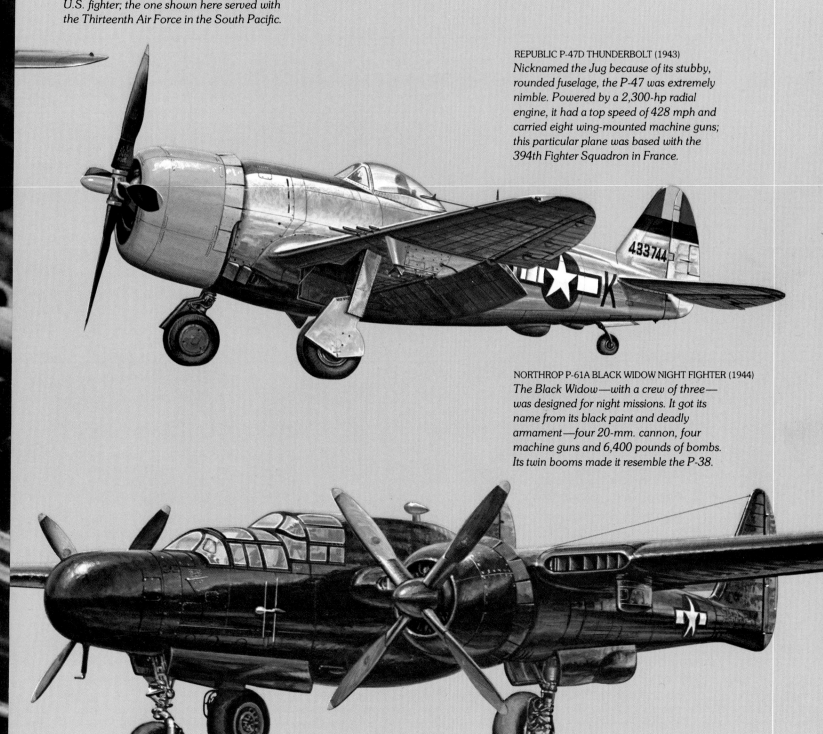

NORTHROP P-61A BLACK WIDOW NIGHT FIGHTER (1944)
*The Black Widow—with a crew of three—
was designed for night missions. It got its
name from its black paint and deadly
armament—four 20-mm. cannon, four
machine guns and 6,400 pounds of bombs.
Its twin booms made it resemble the P-38.*

B-26 Martin Marauders soften up German resistance by scoring a direct hit on a railway bridge across the Rhone River at the city of Arles shortly before

the Allied invasion of southern France in August of 1944.

4

Acme of destruction

General Doolittle's order to the fighter pilots of the Eighth Air Force to pursue the enemy's planes wherever they could find them, going down to strafe them on the ground if necessary, proved the beginning of the final phase of the air war in Europe. The Luftwaffe, once the hunter, was now the hunted. The Eighth's big bomber raids increasingly served two purposes. While the B-17s and 24s bombed Hitler's industries, their escorting fighters were to bleed the Luftwaffe white.

The Eighth's P-47s and 51s were soon joined in these low-level attacks by the swarming fighters of a new air force, the Ninth, which began operating from England during the late autumn of 1943. The Ninth would grow to prodigious size by late spring of the next year. It would have more fighters than the Eighth itself—some 2,000—and rival the Luftwaffe in its heyday as a powerful and efficient ground-support air force.

The Ninth was organized for one vital purpose: to prepare the way for, and then support, Operation *Overlord,* the long-awaited Anglo-American invasion of Europe, targeted for June. The Eighth's big strategic bombers were ill suited for close support of ground actions. The Ninth, equipped with nothing larger than twin-engined mediums, was to give the American air effort a second, tactical punch.

The Ninth had originally been formed in North Africa in 1942 by Major General Lewis H. Brereton, who had commanded the ill-fated Far East Air Force in the Philippines when Japan attacked in December 1941. Brereton's North African force had helped the RAF support the British Eighth Army as it drove the German Afrika Korps out of Egypt and Libya. It had also mounted the famous raid on Ploesti and had supported the Allied invasions of Sicily and Italy. When Brereton was chosen to lead a new Ninth Air Force in Britain—in part because of his experience with the tactical uses of air power—most of the planes and crews of the old Ninth were absorbed into the tactical air force serving in Italy, the Twelfth.

Brereton reached England to assume his new command on October 16, 1943. Fresh equipment was soon pouring in from the States—P-38s, P-47s and P-51s, all to be employed as fighter-bombers, and Douglas A-20 Havoc attack bombers designed for both medium- and low-level missions. Brereton also received a plane as yet little used in Europe, the Martin B-26 Marauder, a swift twin-engined machine suited ace, Gabby Gabreski, would join Johnson and Beeson in prison. While the 56th Group was strafing an airfield near Koblenz, Gabreski, flying very low to get under the enemy ground fire, was astonished to find his propeller gouging chunks of sod from a hillock at the far end of a runway. With its propeller blades bent the Thunderbolt would not lift, so Gabreski slammed its deep, rounded belly into a convenient meadow, tearing a huge furrow as the plane careened to a halt. Unhurt, he scrambled out of the cockpit and sprinted for a nearby wood, where he watched as his circling squadronmates, having seen him escape, shot up and destroyed his new P-47 to keep it from falling into enemy hands.

Gabreski dodged through the German countryside, evading capture for five days, but was finally rounded up by an enemy patrol. When he was marched into a Luftwaffe station to be interrogated, the intelligence officer looked up and said, "Hello Gabby, we've been waiting for you for a long time."

So perilous was the strafing of enemy fields that General Kepner decided to let pilots include planes destroyed on the ground in their records of enemy kills. By that computation, the leading U.S. ace in the European theater was Lieutenant Colonel John C. Meyer of the 352nd Group, who shot down 24 enemy planes and strafed 11 more for a total of 35. Most historians of the War, however, have stuck to the time-honored scheme of counting only planes destroyed in the air, making Gabreski and Bob Johnson the leading American aces in Europe.

The risk of bellying in, the pilots soon found, was higher in a P-51, whose liquid-cooled engine was vulnerable to ground fire. One .30-caliber bullet rupturing a 51's tank of glycol coolant or the tubes through which it circulated would cause the plane's engine to overheat and seize up. The pilot's cockpit was armored and the fuel tanks were self-sealing, but the coolant tank was not, nor was the plumbing in the underside of the fuselage. "Stick a hatpin into the belly of the P-51," a veteran pilot remarked, "and it would bleed to death in five minutes." The weighty Thunderbolt, with its massive air-cooled engine, was not as vulnerable. In consequence, virtually all of the tactical Ninth Air Force's P-51s were eventually transferred to the Eighth, since they shone as escorts, and most of the Eighth's P-47s were reassigned to the Ninth.

As the date for D-Day approached, Brereton's strafing fighters and swift medium bombers continued to beat up 36 airfields between Holland and Brittany, but they also pursued another vital task: destroying the rail lines, roads and bridges leading into Normandy and neighboring Brittany so that the Germans would be unable to send reinforcements to counterattack the Allied landing forces. Putting northwestern Europe's rail system out of commission was a forbidding task in itself. Northern France and Belgium, thickly settled and industrialized, were spider-webbed with thousands of miles of track. Allied intelligence estimated that the Germans could avail themselves of two million freight cars to move troops and supplies to the invasion front.

As the Ninth stepped up these activities in April, its heaviest attacks were concentrated on marshaling yards—often with dramatic results. On April 23, the pilots of a group of P-47s, sent to strike the large yards at Namur in the heart of Belgium, spied the largest concentration of rolling stock they had ever seen. After dropping their bombs on the rail yard, the pilots raced home; within five hours, four groups of B-26s and another group of Thunderbolts were back over the tempting target, hitting hundreds of freight cars and dozens of loaded tank cars.

The Ninth's assault on the railways came to a climax on May 21. So many trains were destroyed that the fliers with oblique humor dubbed the occasion Chattanooga Day, after the popular Glenn Miller recording, "Chattanooga Choo Choo." By late May Brigadier General Elwood R. "Pete" Quesada, head of Brereton's IX Fighter Command, could call on 17 fighter groups—some 1,200 planes—and he sent 11

An anti-U.S. propaganda poster published by the French Vichy government depicts President Roosevelt gloating over the ruins of a bombed city in which a frightened child clutches a doll. More than 67,000 Frenchmen were killed in American and British air attacks during the War.

groups to hit rolling stock north of France's Loire River, which formed the southern border of the area that the Ninth had been ordered to pulverize. The strafing P-47s, P-38s and P-51s claimed 46 locomotives surely destroyed and 32 badly damaged, plus 30 trains shot up and left burning on the tracks.

Quesada's fighters and the Ninth's bomber force varied their targets by also striking at the score of rail and road bridges that crossed the Seine. This river, flowing roughly westward toward the Atlantic from Paris, was the key to isolating the Normandy battlefields. Destroying its bridges would cut off the enemy, since it flowed directly across the routes that German reinforcements attempting to move toward Normandy from the south would be forced to take.

The bridge-busting campaign was so effective that eventually every one of the nine spans crossing the Seine west of Paris was shattered. In all, according to Brereton's diary, 35 bridges were destroyed by the Ninth in the last three weeks before D-Day. This successful campaign, combined with unrelenting destruction of rail and road traffic, effectively sealed off the invasion area from the rest of France, from occupied Belgium and from Germany itself. To make it possible, the Ninth flew 14,000 sorties (a sortie was one flight by one plane) between May 20 and the beginning of June.

As for the two-month campaign against the Luftwaffe's fields, it had been so effective that only 155 single-engined enemy fighters remained in northern France on D-Day and a mere handful showed up to contest the landings—three Focke-Wulf 190s over the invasion armada and after nightfall another 22 aircraft in ineffective attacks on shipping.

D-Day air operations began shortly after midnight, on June 6, as IX Troop Carrier Command dispatched 821 C-47s and C-53s carrying paratroops of the 82nd and 101st Airborne Divisions, and another 104 transports towing gliders loaded with more troops, to their drop zones in France. No fewer than 8,000 planes of the U.S. and Royal Air Forces took part in the assault. Brereton himself was impressed as a section of this flying invasion force took off into the dark at 11-second intervals from the Greenham Common airfield not far from his headquarters. "It was," he noted with satisfaction, "a model of precision flying and discipline."

Once the fleet of transports had crossed the Channel their precision flying suffered from intense German flak, which hit 41 of the transports, and many of the planes lost their way in the predawn darkness, discharging their loads of troopers miles from their intended drop zones. But enough landed on target to capture the most vital crossroads at Ste.-Mère-Église, five miles inland from the beaches.

The transports were followed by the Eighth's formidable bomber fleet. Temporarily diverted from their long-range strategic missions, Doolittle's B-17s and B-24s joined the Ninth in short-range tactical operations. Three huge armadas of four-engined heavies, 1,361 planes

American C-47 transports tow gliders carrying troops of the 82nd and 101st Airborne Divisions over Utah Beach in Normandy during the Allied invasion of Europe on June 6, 1944. The Troop Carrier Command airlifted more than 17,000 men on D-Day with all their guns, ammunition and equipment.

in all, were used to pulverize defenses behind the Normandy beaches. Flying six squadrons abreast, led by radar-equipped pathfinder planes, successive waves of the big bombers dropped nearly 3,000 tons of high explosives through the clouds and mist that wrapped the enemy coastline shortly after dawn.

Brereton soon dispatched the Ninth's 823 bombers and 2,072 fighter-bombers to support the airborne battalions and the first waves of troops scrambling ashore on the invasion beaches through fusillades of enemy fire. One fighter group, the 366th, commanded by Lieutenant Colonel H. Norman Holt, took off from its English airfield as dawn was breaking and headed for the French coast. The 12 P-47s of the squadron with which Holt was flying each carried two 1,000-pound bombs shackled under their wings. Their mission was to knock out a fortified German gun position overlooking Utah Beach.

As the P-47s roared toward their target, Holt had a superb view of the vessels carrying the first waves of Allied troops. "Below us, for a three or four mile stretch, we could pick up innumerable water craft of all sizes, shapes and types. There seemed to be thousands of them. Battleships standing off-shore were firing broadsides over the other craft. Their firepower was helping pin down and hamper return fire from the enemy. At the shoreline, craft were spewing out men and equipment at an astonishing rate. We could see them scattering like kids from school."

As their target came into sight, the three flights of four Thunderbolts each peeled off and dived at the shore battery. The first two wiped it out. The third flight's pilots, already diving, had no option but to fling their bombs into the swirling smoke and debris. Had they not, they might have damaged the planes' wings pulling up with the 1,000-pounders still attached.

Mission accomplished, the squadron checked in by radio with the air controller, code-named "Gimlet," who was directing their part of the D-Day air effort from a battleship in the Channel, asking for another target. Nothing specific, Gimlet informed them; they were to seek out targets of opportunity.

Flying utterly unopposed, Holt and the other Thunderbolt pilots could swoop down to 2,000 feet in flights of four planes and concentrate on a search for other German artillery positions. They spotted one just as its well-concealed gun fired, disturbing the surrounding shrubbery and camouflage nets, thus giving away its location. The P-47s pounced and silenced it with concentrated machine-gun fire.

Without any Luftwaffe planes to fire at, the pilots sprayed their remaining .50-caliber ammunition into wooded areas inland from the invasion beaches, and into the hedgerows bordering the fields and roads that served as screens for enemy troops and artillery. "Unknown to us," Holt realized later, "we were beginning the employment of air coordination right then. It was a logical way to use our armament when the Luftwaffe was conspicuously absent." Even closer coordination between the Ninth's bombing and strafing aircraft and the ground forces would become the rule after D-Day and prove vital to the entire Anglo-American campaign across Europe.

So vital was air support to the success of the landings that many aircraft made several sorties each as the day wore on and some squadrons, short of crews but not machines, sent out planes with partial crews. Setting a record of sorts, a Marauder named *Pickled Dilly* operated with a crew of only three. The pilot, Lieutenant William L. Adams, both flew the B-26 and did his own navigating and radio operation, since the

An infantryman guards the perimeter of a forward airfield in Normandy used by the American Ninth Air Force after D-Day. The Ninth's P-47 fighter-bombers— operating from such temporary bases— flew many thousands of sorties in support of the ground troops, attacking bridges, rail lines and retreating German columns.

copilot, Carl Steen, was forced to substitute for the bombardier, C. W. Holland, who was busy handling the tail guns. *Pickled Dilly* nevertheless put its bombs squarely on target.

A majority of Quesada's fighter groups flew several strikes and some, such as the 404th, got in four full-strength missions between dawn and dusk, totaling 191 sorties. While the Ninth's B-26s and A-20s dropped 419 tons of bombs during the afternoon alone on gun batteries and strategically located bridges and road junctions, the fighters strafed anything that moved among the Normandy hedgerows. So omnipresent were the Allied planes that one German soldier confessed in a letter home, "the American fliers are chasing us like rabbits." In the 24 hours of that fateful day, the 8,000 American and British aircraft participating in the action flew a total of more than 14,600 sorties.

Only hours after the beachheads had been secured, Ninth Air Force engineers bulldozed an emergency airstrip on top of a Normandy headland and by D-plus-8 P-47s were using another hastily built field near Cardonville to provide a close-up version of the air coordination that Colonel Holt began practicing on D-Day. By the end of July, 17 fighter-bomber groups were established at forward fields in France, to be joined soon by the A-20s and B-26s. As the British and American tanks and troops swept across northern Europe, Brereton's engineers performed prodigies, hustling forward in the wake of the advancing armies to construct 70 temporary airfields in France alone.

By June 10, four days after the landings, the Ninth's advanced groups were busy doing two jobs, bombing and strafing German strongpoints at the request of the ground commanders while continuing their vigilant interdiction of rail lines and bridges to seal off the front. On that day the 404th Fighter Group sent 48 P-47s against enemy artillery positions in the morning and hit bridges in the early afternoon. Then late in the day the weary pilots turned their attention to the rail network. One of the group's squadrons, the 507th, spying two approaching supply trains, first cut the tracks in two places, before and behind the trains, and then, with their victims stalled side by side, swooped in to destroy them both with bombs and strafing. Not to be outdone, the 508th attacked the rail hub near Chartres, destroying a switch house, a locomotive and 12 rail cars. The 47s then strafed nearby barracks and set fire to 15 German tanks with their armor-piercing incendiary .50-caliber ammunition.

To keep German engineers from rebuilding the vital bridges over the Seine, the Ninth's bombers attacked the crossing points all through June and July. Five enemy divisions were forced to struggle across the Seine on primitive ferries, and several divisions of reinforcements hastily called in from Holland, Rumania and Russia had to detrain in the Paris area and march to the battlefront. It took one crack division seven days to make a trip of 150 miles; they traveled only at night, since large movements by day inevitably attracted swarms of strafing planes. The 9th and 10th SS Panzer Divisions were forced to detrain at Versailles and other points west of Paris and march under cover of darkness along secondary roads, taking two weeks to reach the front.

Some German outfits never got there. On July 11, the inaptly code-named "Slipshod Blue" flight of the 366th Fighter Group, having failed to find its assigned pillbox targets, suddenly perceived below 50 or 60 enemy tanks that, shielded by a light rain, were driving hard toward the Allied lines near St.-Lô. Slipshod Blue leader immediately radioed the formation leader, "Rupert," then made a pass at the tanks to indicate their position.

Rupert quickly marshaled his forces, instructing the "Slipshod Red" and "Yellow" flights to follow Blue flight in on the target and pulling two other squadrons, "Relic" and "Foxhunt," into the line of attack. "Take time," Rupert cautioned. "Make every bomb and bullet count."

One after another the Thunderbolts dropped their bombs, then went down to 100 feet and, despite heavy ground fire, strafed the tanks. Scattering for cover, the tanks became even easier prey: A third of the column was knocked out in 20 minutes. The P-47s then flew back to their nearby field, rearmed and hustled back to strike again. This time, the 366th left 35 tanks burning just 200 yards from the Allied lines. By afternoon the rain was heavy, but there was no stopping the excited pilots; they made a third foray, spotted another

A big warbird called the Liberator

CONSOLIDATED B-24H LIBERATOR HEAVY BOMBER (1943)
Powered by four 1,200-hp Pratt & Whitney radial engines, the B-24H had 10 defensive machine guns and a top speed of 290 mph. This one, named Also Ran, flew with the Eighth Air Force's 467th Bomber Group based in Norfolk, England.

The Consolidated B-24 Liberator was built in greater numbers than any other American plane of the War. From 1941 onward, 18,188 of these heavy bombers rolled off U.S. assembly lines in more than a dozen different models—the B-24H shown here and in a cutaway on the following page appeared in 1943.

Designed in 1939, the B-24 embodied all the technical advances that had occurred since the debut of the Boeing B-17 in 1934. It was not, however, in the words of one pilot, "the shapely, romantic beauty some of its contemporaries were. It looked like a truck, it hauled big loads like a truck and it flew like a truck."

But with an 8,800-pound bombload and a 2,100-mile range, the ungainly, twin-finned B-24 was an excellent truck at a time when trucks were badly needed. Its stubby fuselage had an eight-foot-high bomb bay that could hold as many as a dozen 500-pound bombs stowed horizontally. The bomb-bay doors were built into the sides of the fuselage and slid open from beneath like a roll-top desk. A catwalk traversed the bomb bay to enable the crew to move about.

The B-24's most distinctive feature was its 110-foot-long, deceptively slender wing, which housed 18 tanks holding 2,364 gallons of fuel and the main landing gear, which folded up between the engines. But its special high-lift airfoils lost their efficiency above 24,000 feet or when the plane was flown at the lower speeds often needed to keep formation. The result was an unstable, mushing progress—one flier likened it to "a fat lady doing a ballet"—that made the B-24 notoriously hard to handle. Most Liberator pilots and air crews took the challenge in stride, however. Said one, "We felt it was an accomplishment to fly it."

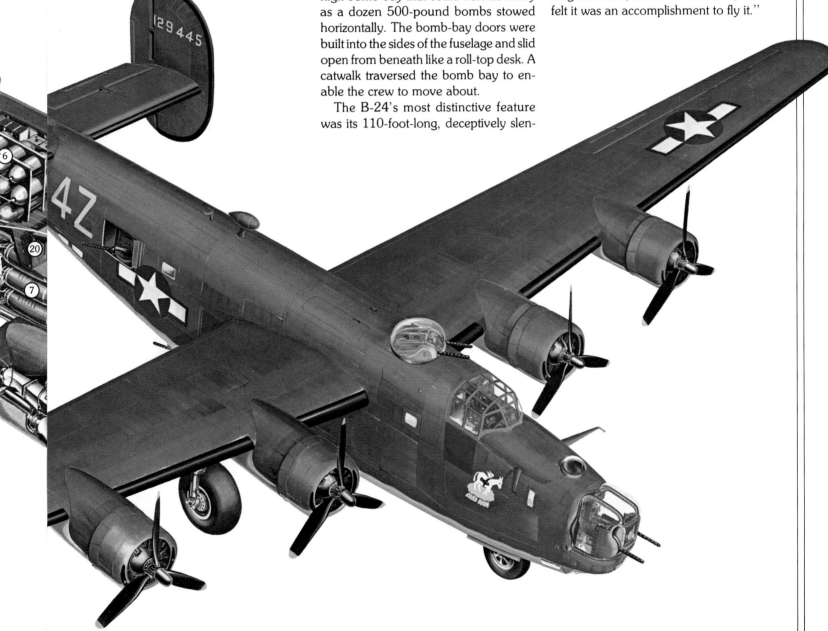

using only bomb-carrying fighters, to rest his bomber crews and surprise the enemy, but the refineries remained a tough target. Not until its last attack into Rumania, on August 19, did the Fifteenth get off scot-free, with no losses. By then the campaign had cost 223 planes. The Rumanian refineries, however, were now little more than a collection of burned-out storage tanks and twisted pipes.

The oil campaign had a swift and devastating effect on the Luftwaffe. Because of the lack of fuel, the training of new Luftwaffe pilots was radically curtailed and they went into battle after only some 30 hours of flying time. The green pilots proved no match for the experienced Mustang, Lightning and Thunderbolt pilots who had had more than 300 hours in the air before being assigned to operational units. Luftwaffe interceptions of the bomber streams from England and Italy became intermittent, since fuel had to be hoarded in order to assemble a large enough formation of fighters to effectively tackle the bombers. The Forts and Liberators increasingly seemed to roam the skies over Germany unchallenged, a majority of losses coming not from fighters but from flak. Heavy escorts were less and less necessary, which released yet more fighters to beat up enemy airfields. "We were almost reduced to immobility," Luftwaffe fighter chief Galland wrote, "by continuous raids on our airfields."

The planes of the Ninth, continuing their close ground-support missions as the U.S. armies raced across northern France and the Low Countries, were so deadly that German troops on occasion surrendered rather than suffer further attacks from the omnipresent P-47s. Several hundred gave themselves up to a squadron of the 405th Fighter Group while its Thunderbolts were strafing trucks northeast of Le Mans in mid-August. As the pilots prepared to make another attack, they spotted German soldiers waving white flags. Then, as the pilots buzzed the troops but held their fire, the Germans below, still waving white flags, fell into a column and began marching toward the nearest American lines. The American infantry, warned by radio of what was happening, gleefully received the surrendering force.

A far larger body surrendered after being ceaselessly harried by General Weyland's XIX Tactical Command. This was a force 20,000 strong that had found itself just south of the Loire River when Patton's Third Army began its dash toward Paris. The German commander, Major General Eric Elster, was in position to cross the Loire and attack Patton's exposed right flank, but he found that Weyland's fighter-bombers pounced immediately whenever he began to move troops or vehicles into position for an assault. His losses mounting with his frustration, Elster capitulated on September 16. Weyland had the curious experience, for an air commander, of being present at a surrender ceremony during which an entire ground army laid down its arms.

At just the time General Elster was giving up, Patton's spearheads were grinding to a halt, his tanks out of fuel and his troops running short

The Fifteenth's Red Tail Angels

Captain Armour G. McDaniels of the 301st Squadron points out a cannon hole in his P-51 to ground crewmen after an escort mission late in the War. Shot down over Berlin in 1945, he was taken prisoner and eventually freed by advancing Allied troops.

To bomber crews of the Fifteenth Air Force—who owed them a particular debt—the men of the four squadrons of the 332nd Fighter Group, the 99th, 100th, 301st and 302nd, were the Red Tail Angels. Flying P-51 Mustangs with tails painted vermilion, they had by the end of the War won for themselves the distinction of not only having damaged or destroyed some 400 enemy aircraft, but of never having lost one of the bombers they escorted on missions over Europe—a rare achievement.

Recognition of their abilities had come slowly. The pilots were all black, graduates of the Army Air Forces Flying Training Program at Tuskegee, Alabama. The Air Corps only reluctantly admitted the first black flying cadets in 1941 and—like other black servicemen—they remained segregated throughout the War.

The first all-black unit to go overseas was the 99th Squadron, which arrived at Fordjouna, North Africa, in May of 1943.

It was led by an iron-willed West Point graduate, Lieutenant Colonel Benjamin O. Davis Jr., who had been the first black officer to earn pilot's wings. "There was constantly before us the challenge," he later wrote, "to refute the widely accepted belief that Blacks could not learn to fly airplanes or participate successfully in combat operations."

Davis drove his men relentlessly, and the payoff came on July 2, when Lieutenant Charles Hall, in one of the P-40 Warhawks the squadron was then flying, scored the unit's first kill by shooting down a German FW 190 over Sicily during a bomber escort mission. The following month, Davis was ordered to return to the States to take command of three more all-black squadrons—then completing their training at Selfridge Field, Michigan—and to bring them back to the Mediterranean, where he formed the 332nd Group, incorporating his old command, the 99th Squadron.

In the final months of the War, the 332nd was based at Ramitelli, Italy. On the 24th of March, 1945, Davis, with 72 of his planes, escorted a formation of the Fifteenth Air Force's bombers on a 1,600-mile round-trip attack on Berlin. The 332nd was supposed to turn back short of the target after being relieved by another fighter group. But when they arrived over the city's outskirts, no other fighters appeared. Davis ordered his men to press on.

Minutes later, the formation was set upon by jet-powered Messerschmitt 262 fighters and a vicious dogfight ensued: The 332nd, its Mustangs now dangerously low on fuel, fought off the attackers, shooting down three of the German jets and losing two of their own planes, including that of the commander of the 301st Squadron, Captain Armour G. McDaniels *(above)*. For its valiant action that day, the group was awarded a Distinguished Unit Citation.

of ammunition and food. As November and December came, one of the coldest and stormiest winters in memory grounded the Ninth Air Force's A-20s, B-26s and P-47s nearly half the time.

Seeing the Allied ground forces stalled and air power immobilized, Hitler concocted a last-ditch counterattack through the Ardennes Forest, a lightly held section of the First Army's front at a point where the borders of Belgium and Luxembourg meet. Under cover of the bad weather, Field Marshal Gerd von Rundstedt assembled some eight panzer and 10 infantry divisions. Unhappily for the U.S. ground troops, aerial photographs taken by the few reconnaissance planes that braved the weather were not correctly interpreted by intelligence experts, who failed to detect the enemy build-up in the snow-blanketed forest. The panzers lunged forward on December 16 and punched a great swollen salient in the First Army's front. The Battle of the Bulge was on.

For a week continuing foul weather hampered the Allied air forces in their attempts to intervene. But at last, on December 23, a cold front spreading over northern Europe brought clear skies. The Ninth's fighter-bombers attacked the enemy tanks and infantry with fury while its C-47s began flying in supplies for the embattled forward units—including the 101st Airborne, which was trapped at Bastogne.

The close support that the beleaguered 101st got from the Ninth's P-47s was probably more welcome than the supplies. For five days, from dawn on December 23 to dusk on the 27th, the Thunderbolts of the 406th Group strafed and bombed every gun position, vehicle, tank and enemy-held building within 10 miles of Bastogne. At the same time, the Ninth's mediums went after the Coblenz rail yards and other communications centers behind the German lines, seeking to cut off deliveries of supplies to Rundstedt's panzers.

The Marauders and Havocs paid an unexpectedly high price for these raids. The Luftwaffe had been husbanding planes and fuel and suddenly sent out 800 fighter sorties, inflicting the highest losses ever suffered by the Ninth's bombers in a single day. Of the 624 mediums sent to strike key rail yards and bridges near the front, 40 were shot down, two crash-landed and 182 were crippled, some so badly that they would never fly again.

The Luftwaffe's triumph was short-lived. On the next day, the Eighth Air Force and the RAF, combining forces, sent 2,834 heavies to hit every airfield and communications center in the region, and on Christmas Day 422 heavies and 629 mediums continued the pounding. With all available Luftwaffe support eliminated, Rundstedt's columns had no cover whatsoever and they began to melt away under the Allied air and ground assault. Hitler's counterattack, which was to have reversed the fortunes of the War, swiftly fizzled out.

Unchastened by this costly last-ditch measure, Hitler ordered Reich Marshal Göring to launch his own offensive on New Year's Day. Having hastily collected some 700 planes in western Germany, most flown by green pilots, Göring ordered them aloft en masse to bomb and strafe the

Smoke billows from 13 Stuka dive bombers hit on the ground by Ninth Air Force Thunderbolts. Bombing and strafing for 40 minutes, the P-47s destroyed 24 planes and crippled another 20. The Luftwaffe aircraft had been getting ready to strike the U.S.-held bridge over the Rhine at Remagen.

Allied forward fields in Belgium and the Netherlands. The sudden onslaught took the British and American fliers by surprise, but they reacted with murderous swiftness. "The enemy was engaged immediately by a flight of eight of our T-bolts that had just taken off and assembled," recalled Colonel Holt. "They attacked the enemy planes and kept them from hitting our pitifully unprotected planes on the ground. The entire air circus took place at tree-top level directly over the strip."

One squadron commander, Holt remembered, "leaped out of the sack to get in on the kills" and flew in his pajamas. "Me 109s and FW 190s were flaming and augering into the ground" within sight of the field. In the end, Holt's P-47 group, the 366th, shot down 12 German planes, and the Mustang-equipped 352nd, based on the same Belgian field, knocked down 23. Ground fire accounted for seven more, for a total of 42 destroyed of the 50 that had attacked. The 366th lost one plane, but the pilot survived, racing back to the field on a bicycle from where his plane had bellied in and yelling, "They got me, but I got two of them first!"

Not every Allied field escaped as lightly as Holt's; 156 American and RAF planes were destroyed, mostly on the ground. But the Luftwaffe sacrificed at least 200 aircraft in Hitler's foolhardy assault. "The enemy had come charging out of his corner," Holt said, "only to be smacked to his knees." After such losses of planes and pilots, the German air force ceased to be an effective force; virtually the only sound in the skies over Europe was the drone of the heavy bombers of the Eighth and Fifteenth as they continued strategic operations, and the roar of the Ninth's low-flying bombers and strafers as they prepared the way for the final drive into Germany by the ground forces.

By March 20, 1945, the Allied armies were gathering on the Rhine, their largest spearheads moving toward a position opposite a town named Wesel. To make sure the remnants of the Luftwaffe would not interfere with the river crossings, the Eighth sent out 1,254 bombers on March 21 to hit 10 airfields in northwestern Germany and it pounded five more the next day. On the 23rd the B-17s and 24s were back, pulverizing marshaling yards in the Ruhr, cutting rail traffic to the region around Wesel. But the most intensive bombing was reserved for Wesel itself. In a carpet bombing reminiscent of that at St.-Lô, the town was flattened into a lunar landscape; almost nothing was left.

The advance of the ground armies on March 24 was aided by the largest airborne assault on record as 14,365 parachute and glider troops were ferried over the Rhine by so many transports that the stream of planes as it approached the German frontier was 420 miles long. The airborne infantry, supported by Allied fighters and bombers flying 7,000 sorties, quickly fanned out to capture Wesel and the surrounding area while the ground armies built temporary bridges over the Rhine and began pouring equipment across them.

On the next day, the fighter-bomber claims reached staggering proportions as the planes launched another interdiction campaign, sealing off the battlefield to enemy reinforcements and supplies. The P-47s and 51s destroyed 76 locomotives, 858 railway cars, 742 motor- and 76 horse-drawn vehicles, 69 tanks and 49 other armored vehicles. They severed rail lines in 47 places, blasted 25 highways, knocked out 27 gun positions and demolished 133 buildings, seven factories, four warehouses, four hangars, two roundhouses, and at least one barge, bridge, supply dump, radio station, ammunition dump and switch house. The Luftwaffe could not respond to this merciless pounding. A bitter joke that circulated among some German antiaircraft gunners perhaps best describes the situation: "If a plane is silvery looking, it's American; if it's dark in color, it's British; if it can't be seen at all, it's German."

On April 16 the long strategic air war officially came to an end; there were no more targets. By then the big bombers of the Eighth, the Fifteenth and the RAF had destroyed 100 per cent of Germany's coke and ferroalloy industries; 95 per cent of its fuel, hard coal and synthetic rubber capacity; 90 per cent of its steel capacity; 75 per cent of its truck manufacturing; 70 per cent of its tire production; and 55 per cent of its tank manufacturing. In the course of the air war, the Eighth's fighters alone had strafed into wreckage 4,250 Luftwaffe planes—to add to their score of about 5,222 shot from the air. Two senior fighter groups, the 4th and 56th, both ran their records to more than 1,000 enemy aircraft destroyed.

As crushing as the air victory was, it had been costly. In three years the Eighth and Ninth Air Forces had lost 48,847 air crew killed or missing in action and presumed dead, and the Eighth a staggering 3,908 planes destroyed. "Except for the infantry, always the hardest hit," General Arnold wrote, "no group in the Army, in the air or on the ground, including paratroops and armored divisions, suffered as high a casualty rate as did our heavy bomber crews over Germany."

The ground armies swiftly conquered the rest of the Reich as the tactical air forces continued their destructive campaign. One Third Army officer described a road in southwestern Germany where the heavy equipment of what appeared to be a division had been "caught in a defile and massacred" by fighter-bombers. "Running down the curving roadway, the passer-by first notices a few scattered vehicles and dead horses," the officer reported, "then it seems to grow in crescendo until finally he is in the midst of such a twisted mass of death and destruction that single items no longer stand out. The only impression made is that this is the acme and ultimate of death, destruction and chaos."

If he did not venture forth from his refuge in Austria to witness this horrible reality for himself, Reich Marshal Hermann Göring, the man who had commanded the once-illustrious Luftwaffe, knew all too well the key reason behind Germany's crushing defeat. "The Allies owe the success of the invasion to the air forces," Göring confessed. "They prepared the invasion; they made it possible; they carried it through. Without the U.S. air force, the war would still be going on elsewhere, but certainly not on German soil." ⌇

Craters and burned-out buildings are all that remain of

Wesel, Germany, after American bombers pulverized the Rhine River city to clear the way for the landing of 14,365 airborne troops on March 24, 1945.

America's king of the air

Cadet Bong reports for training in California in May 1941.

Although General George Kenney had once reprimanded "that stunt-flying bad boy" for buzzing a friend's home in California, he made Richard Ira Bong his first pick when forming a new P-38 fighter squadron in the southwest Pacific in the fall of 1942. Bong did not disappoint him: In 146 missions between September 1942 and December 1944, the farm boy from Poplar, Wisconsin, piled up 40 kills to become America's highest-scoring ace.

Never a great marksman, Bong developed his own technique for making kills. He would swoop down on his targets and blast them at dangerously close range, then pull up fast.

After his 40th kill, Bong was ordered home by Kenney. Stateside, he began testing P-80 jets for the Air Forces. An accident, after just four hours of flight time in the new aircraft, cost Bong his life. He died the day the atomic bomb fell on Hiroshima.

At Hamilton Field, California, Bong (far left in the back row) stands with squadronmates in front of a P-38 fighter they flew there.

Bong manages a grin in New Guinea, where, he said, there was "nothing but mosquitoes and movies to entertain you."

The budding ace prepares for takeoff in his P-38. Bong praised the Lightning for its "big firepower wallop" and ability to climb "like a homesick angel."

Bong's gun camera records his ninth victory—a Japanese Dinah reconnaissance bomber—in March 1943.

Newsmen pester Bong, eager for details of his aerial victories. Modestly, he often would credit the skill of his wingmen.

A hometown hero's welcome

Back home on his first leave after 21 victories, Captain Bong strolls with an admiring flock through tiny Poplar in November 1943.

Down at Grymala's grocery, the ace shoots craps with George Renquist (left) and Charlie Smith, a hand on the Bong farm.

Renowned as a trencherman, Bong sits down to a long-awaited home-cooked meal with his family and a visiting reporter.

Bong, who got his first rifle at the age of 12, shows off the bucks he and an uncle bagged.

Visiting Wisconsin's capitol, Bong tries out the Governor's desk.

Bong buzzes the shipyards in Superior where earlier he was named "Number One Pin-Up Boy" by the "Welderettes."

In the summer of 1944, Dick joins crooner Bing Crosby in a "Bing-Bong" routine at a Hollywood war loan concert.

The sweet taste of victory

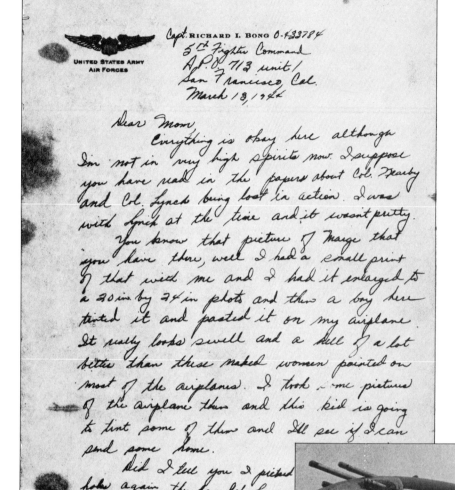

Capt. RICHARD I. BONG 0-433784
5th Fighter Command
A.P.O. 713 unit 1
San Francisco, Cal.
March 13, 1944

Dear Mom,

Everything is okay here although I'm not in very high spirits now. I suppose you have read in the papers about Col. Wearby and Col. Lynch being lost in action. I was with Lynch at the time and it wasn't pretty.

You know that picture of Marge that you have there, well I had a small print of that with me and I had it enlarged to a 20 in. by 24 in. photo and then a boy here tinted it and pasted it on my airplane. It really looks swell and a hell of a lot better than these naked women painted on most of the airplanes. I took some pictures of the airplane then and this kid is going to tint some of them and I'll see if I can send some home.

Did I tell you I [...]

Bong compares notes with ace Tom McGuire, who, when eight kills shy of Bong's record, tagged himself Eight-Behind McGuire.

In a letter to his mother, Dick tells her how he pasted a picture of Marge Vattendahl, his girl back home, on his P-38 (right). "It really looks swell," he added, "and a hell of a lot better than these naked women painted on most of the airplanes."

Clasping Bong's shoulders, General Douglas MacArthur inducts the ace into "the society of the bravest of the brave, the wearers of the Medal of Honor."

Bong escorts his bride, Marge, from Superior's Concordia Lutheran Church on February 10, 1945, just six months before he was killed.

Two Superfortresses — used in the air battle against Japan — sit on a hastily cleared field on Guam in late 1944 as a bulldozer widens the runway.

5

"One damned island after another"

In a straight line the distance between Hawaii and the Japanese mainland," General George Kenney once noted longingly, "measures 2,544 miles"—a mere 15-hour round trip for a fast airplane.

The problem was, as Kenney well knew, that no World War II bomber could make operational round-trip flights of such length. In Europe the U.S. Air Forces had a most convenient platform—England—from which to bombard the enemy; Berlin was 500 miles from East Anglia. But in the Pacific the distances were immense—and at first the Japanese controlled all the platforms, all the island airstrips from which bombers could reach Tokyo.

The entire Pacific campaign was a process of trying to lever the enemy from his widespread outposts one by one. The strategy concocted by Kenney and General MacArthur, and the similar one used by Admiral Chester Nimitz, who was in charge of the Navy's island-hopping campaigns, depended on air power. Aircraft were to pound the successive Japanese strongholds, softening them up for invasion by ground troops. After an outpost was secured, airfields would be built from which bombers could go on to attack the next enemy enclave.

The U.S. Navy and its Marines were assigned the job of clearing the tiny and widely scattered coral outcrops of the central Pacific—places with such names as Tarawa and Kwajalein and Saipan. For the purpose they were given the backing of a small Army air force, the Seventh. Making long overwater flights to bombard one tiny island after another was a tedious and thankless job for the Seventh; its planes flew, in the words of its unit history, "the longest missions in the world against the smallest targets."

In another thrust to the south, the Navy, aided by the Thirteenth Air Force, was to drive through the Solomon Islands with Marines and borrowed Army divisions, removing the enemy threat to northern Australia before pushing on toward Japan via the Philippines and Formosa.

Kenney's Fifth Air Force, with Australian and American ground troops commanded by MacArthur, would deliver the left hook, pushing the Japanese out of the largest of the islands, New Guinea, and from New Britain before going on to Morotai in the Moluccas on a southerly route to the Philippines.

The Pacific war differed greatly from the European campaigns. "Tanks and heavy artillery can be reserved for the battlefields of Europe

the only fighters with sufficient range to make the 435-mile flight from Henderson Field on Guadalcanal in the lower Solomons to Bougainville at the northern end of the chain. On April 18, in a marvel of pinpoint navigation and timing, 16 Lightnings led by Major John W. Mitchell arrived over Kahili just as Yamamoto's Mitsubishi bomber and its escorting Zekes hove into view. Mitchell took a dozen of the P-38s up to 20,000 feet to occupy the top escort while Captain Thomas G. Lanphier led the rest of the Lightnings in the attack on Yamamoto's plane.

Lanphier and his wingman, Lieutenant Rex Barber, were within two miles of Yamamoto's plane when they saw the Zekes of the low-flying escort jettison their belly tanks to lighten their planes for combat. Surprise was gone. "They nosed over in a group," Lanphier recalled, "and we closed in fast. The three nearest Zekes dived toward us, and then the three from the other side. My machine guns and cannon ripped the wing away from the first and he twisted under me, all flame and smoke. His two wing men hurtled past.

"I kicked my plane over on its back and looked down for the lead Jap bomber," Lanphier remembered. He soon spotted it, "skimming above the jungle, heading for Kahili. The bomber was too close to the ground for the men to bail out. I put a long, steady burst into the right engine, then the right wing, and saw it break into flame. Just as I came into range of its tail cannon, the wing tore off and the plane plunged into the jungle and exploded."

The loss of Yamamoto, the great naval-aerial strategist, would have devastating consequences. Japan had no one else of his stature or wisdom to direct either its Navy or air weapons, which henceforth would be increasingly outmaneuvered by American forces.

By the early summer of 1943 Kenney was ready to start hitting the Japanese airfields around Lae and Salamaua on New Guinea's Huon Gulf. His aim was to knock out the enemy air force there and prepare the way for amphibious and airborne assaults that would begin on June 30 and were designed to secure the area by September. The 350-mile round trip from Buna to Lae was a long haul for fighters, however, cutting into the time they could remain over the target. With characteristic daring, Kenney set up two forward airfields near a jungle outpost called Marilinan, only 60 miles inland from Lae, flying in the engineers and equipment needed to construct the strips. These airfields—which the Japanese did not discover until they were completed—also gave Kenney's fighters the range to reach Wewak, farther westward on the New Guinea coast, where, by August, the Japanese had established a force of some 225 aircraft. Kenney decided to try to annihilate these enemy planes before they could attack his own airfields.

On August 17, some 41 B-24s plus a dozen of the Fifth's battle-weary B-17s hit all of the four airdromes in the vicinity, including Wewak itself. The primary mission of this first wave was to knock out the Japa-

The Pacific war's well-kept secret

News of the death of Admiral Isoroku Yamamoto, the planner of Pearl Harbor and one of Japan's greatest military tacticians, could have boosted U.S. morale, but it was concealed. If it had been announced that his plane had been shot down, the Japanese would have realized their code had been broken—there was no other way the Americans could have known Yamamoto was on board.

But the U.S. government had an additional reason for keeping news of Yamamoto's death quiet. The brother of Captain Thomas G. Lanphier, one of the two P-38 pilots who had destroyed the plane, was a prisoner of the Japanese, and officials feared for his life.

ADMIRAL ISOROKU YAMAMOTO

The bullet-riddled wreck of Admiral Yamamoto's Mitsubishi bomber lies where it fell in the Bougainville jungle on April 18, 1943.

nese antiaircraft guns and generally disrupt the airfields' defenses.

The next wave consisted of B-25s modified to include eight or more forward-firing machine guns in their noses. Lieutenant Colonel Donald Hall, a veteran of the earlier campaign for Buna, led the Mitchells in a line-abreast attack on the Borum airfield. "Coming in over the tops of the palm trees, Don saw a sight to gladden the heart of a strafer," Kenney wrote in his memoirs. "The Jap bombers, 60 of them, were lined up on either side of the runway with their engines turning over, flying crews on board, and groups of ground crewmen standing by each airplane. The Japs were actually starting to take off and the leading airplane was already halfway down the runway and ready to leave the ground." At this point Hall opened fire and blew up the first Japanese bomber. It crashed, blocking the runway. The rest of the B-25s then scythed across the field, setting fire to the double line of bombers with .50-caliber incendiaries and a rain of parafrag bombs. The Japanese planes began to self-destruct as the bombs in their bomb bays detonated.

Virtually the same thing took place on the Wewak airfield, where 30 Japanese fighters were warming up for takeoff. Though only 12 Mitchells swept the strip, they all but annihilated the enemy fighters. An even smaller force of three B-25s managed to attack Dagua—the weather was closing in—but those three, by Kenney's estimate, destroyed 20 Japanese planes and damaged 20 more. After the War Japanese records revealed that Kenney's strafers on August 17 destroyed more than 150 aircraft. All of the B-25s and their escort, some 80 P-38s, returned safely to base.

On August 18 General Whitehead, Kenney's deputy, staged an even more devastating raid on Wewak. Twenty-six B-24s and B-17s dropped 100 tons of bombs on the fields and they were followed immediately by 53 twin-engined strafers. Japanese fighters came up to attack the Americans and this time shot down three B-25s and one P-38, but they could not prevent the almost total destruction of the Japanese planes that had not taken off. In addition, the P-38s and the bomber gunners, according to Kenney, shot down 32 of the Zeros that had

In the photographs below, an A-20, caught by antiaircraft fire after hitting the Japanese supply center at Kokas, Dutch New Guinea, dives to its doom in the MacCluer Gulf while the accompanying wingman escapes. The plane from which these pictures were taken returned to its Hollandia, New Guinea, base peppered with more than 100 machine-gun and shrapnel holes.

intercepted. "During the two days' operations," Kenney wrote, "we had destroyed on the ground and in the air practically the entire Japanese air force in the Wewak area."

Kenney's campaign to gain mastery of the air over New Guinea provided his fighter pilots in their heavily armed P-38s and P-47s with excellent opportunities to fatten their scores. Among Kenney's "kids"—as he called all his men—was a young captain from Pennsylvania named Thomas J. Lynch, who was known for his slashing fighter tactics. Leading a formation of 12 Lightnings from the 49th Group sent up to protect Dobodura, a U.S. airfield near Buna, from enemy attack, Lynch came upon a formation of seven Japanese dive bombers escorted by at least 20 Zeros. Splitting his dozen planes into three flights of four to gain maneuverability, Lynch dived with his squadron straight into the Japanese formation.

Three Zeros had maneuvered onto the tail of a P-38 when Lynch swept in, blew up one Zero and chased the other two off. He looked around, spotted another enemy plane and, after a single good burst, watched it splash into the sea. Out of ammunition, he headed back for his home base at Port Moresby, hoping to borrow another P-38 and return to the battle, but before he could, his squadronmates had put the Japanese to flight, claiming a total of seven Zeros shot down, plus two Aichi Val dive bombers and a pair of Oscars (Nakajima fighters).

Another of Kenney's kids was 31-year-old Colonel Neel Kearby, the commander of the 348th Fighter Group. The 348th, equipped with P-47s, was the first to fly Thunderbolts in the Pacific. The hulking Jug was initially looked upon with suspicion by pilots who had flown the P-40 or the P-38. Kearby proved that the P-47 was a powerful weapon, its eight machine guns seeming to shred the flimsy Japanese planes.

Kearby's group became operational in August 1943, during the campaign to eliminate Wewak. The hunting was excellent; by the end of September Kearby had destroyed eight Japanese aircraft. Shortly after that, on October 11, as the campaign neared its close, Kearby had his biggest day, knocking down six planes.

The October mission began as a routine precautionary sweep. Re-

connaissance photographs had shown that only seven serviceable Japanese planes remained on the airstrips around Wewak; Kenney nevertheless had kept the area under surveillance in the belief that the Japanese might be camouflaging their true strength. Kearby and his three wingmen found that Kenney's suspicions were justified.

Arriving over Wewak at 28,000 feet, the Americans first encountered a single Zeke, which they shot down after a brief battle. Then Kearby spotted "about 36 fighters, Zekes, Hamps and Tonys, at 10,000 feet approaching from the east," evidently recently arrived reinforcements sent west from Rabaul. "Our P-47s came in from above on a Zeke, opened fire at 1,500 feet and closed as he burst into flame."

Without pausing, Kearby turned "and opened fire on a Hamp at 1,500 feet from seven o'clock. He burst into flame." Kearby then "looked up and another Hamp was turning slightly above and from about eight o'clock." Kearby quickly flamed this one also, with a short burst of fire from his P-47's eight guns.

The Japanese pilots, now aware of the source of these swift attacks, turned toward the small group of P-47s. Rather than face more than 30 angry enemy aviators, the Americans started for home. "Immediately at two o'clock below at about 20,000 feet I saw a P-47 with one Tony about 3,000 feet to the rear and another about 3,000 feet behind the first one. I turned and came in at 400 miles per hour on the tail of the rear Tony, opening fire at 1,500 feet. He took no evasive action and burst into flame."

Kearby immediately flamed the second—"I opened fire from about 2,000 feet closing in and saw tracers going into him and pieces of his wing and fuselage flying off"—and then called his flight together for a dash back to their home base. In the battle, during which they had been outnumbered by more than 8 to 1, Kearby and his three wingmen had accounted for nine Japanese aircraft. Kearby's feat of destroying six was rewarded with the Medal of Honor.

With the Wewak airfields pulverized, Kenney and Whitehead turned their attention to Rabaul, the source of all Japanese reinforcements heading for New Guinea. An all-out assault began on October 12 as 114 B-25s, aided by a dozen twin-engined Beaufighters flown by Royal Australian Air Force pilots, hit the airfields in the vicinity of the big enemy base, catching some 270 planes on the ground; 100 were destroyed and 51 damaged. The mediums also hit fuel and ammunition dumps, causing explosions and fires. Then more than 80 B-24s attacked the shipping in Rabaul's Simpson Harbour with devastating effect. The P-38s that escorted the raid claimed to have shot down 26 Zeros out of the 35 or so that had taken off. By this time in the Pacific war American fighter pilots were clearly outclassing the opposition. Many of the experienced Japanese pilots, meticulously trained before the War, had been shot down and their replacements were hastily trained and green.

This raid was merely a rehearsal for the attack of November 2, which,

Kenney said, could be compared in its destructiveness to the Bismarck Sea Battle. Both B-25s and P-38s first swept in at low level to machine-gun the Japanese antiaircraft positions, dropping Kenney cocktails, 100-pound phosphorous bombs, as they went. Then more B-25s, under the command of a burly ex-Notre Dame football player named Jock Henebry, went into Simpson Harbour at mast height, skip-bombing the ships at anchor. Fire from the deck guns of the Japanese vessels was fierce, but Henebry's 41 planes scored hits on 30 vessels out of the 38 lying in the anchorage.

As the B-25s zoomed up, they were attacked by some 150 Japanese fighters. The battle was furious. Six B-25s were shot down. Henebry's plane was riddled but managed to stagger away from Rabaul and crash into the sea; he and his crew, along with four P-38 pilots who had also ditched shot-up aircraft, were picked up by Navy rescue seaplanes. Kenney's total loss was 20 aircraft, a high figure for the Fifth, but the Japanese losses were far higher. More than 60 fighters had been shot down and another 17 demolished on the ground. Moreover, the attack on Simpson Harbour accounted for 114,000 tons of shipping sunk or damaged. This devastating raid was followed several days later by another attack by a combined force of carrier-based U.S. Navy planes and land-based bombers.

With MacArthur's forces safely in control of the Lae-Salamaua area and Finschhafen to the north on the Huon Peninsula, Kenney could begin softening up Cape Gloucester, the ground forces' next objective, in December 1943. With Cape Gloucester taken, MacArthur's right flank would be secure. In addition, airfields built on the cape would put Kenney's planes so close to Japanese-held Rabaul, on the other end of New Britain, that it could not be used as a main base and its isolated garrison could be left to die on the vine.

The devastation wrought on the cape by Kenney's bombers added a new term to the Fifth Air Force's glossary: "Gloucesterizing." Reconnaissance flights revealed that about 5,000 Japanese troops were building defensive positions along the shore in expectation of an American amphibious landing. Kenney's ambition was to enable the Marines that were scheduled go ashore on the cape to do so without having to fire a shot. To that end his heavies and mediums dropped more than 4,000 tons of bombs on Japanese positions between December 1 and Christmas Day, plastering airfields, supply dumps and the artillery positions and machine-gun nests along the beaches. On Christmas Eve radar-equipped B-24s cruised over the area, in the words of a Fifth Air Force historian, "dropping bombs and tossing out grenades, beer bottles, and anything else that would make the Japanese miserable and sleepless." On the morning of December 26th, Kenney noted with pride that the 1st Marine Division had landed, as he had predicted, "with their rifles on their backs."

Not every Fifth Air Force operation went as smoothly as the Wewak

in New Guinea, in preparation for its seizure by MacArthur's troops.

Despite threatening weather, Kenney ordered the important strike to go ahead as planned. More than 130 bombers—B-24s, B-25s and A-20s, with 40 P-38 escorts—struck hard, smashing the enemy's fixed defenses and driving the Japanese troops into the jungle.

Visibility over Hollandia, on New Guinea's northern coast, was fine, but as the formations tried to fly back eastward toward their bases in the Lae-Salamaua area, they found their normal route down the Markham valley blocked by fog and low clouds. The clouds, in the words of one P-38 pilot, sealed the valley's mouth "as neatly as a black and white block of cement."

The fighters were running low on fuel, and with the weather front looming ahead they knew they were cut off from home. Some of the bombers and most of the P-38s pulled out of the Markham valley and headed toward an emergency strip at Saidor on the coast. It too was socked in, but ground crews at the strip turned on an electronic homing device to guide the planes in. As the aviators struggled to follow the beacon toward Saidor, the air crackled with expletives and exclamations and all standard landing procedures went out the window. One B-24 made it to the runway only to find that a P-38 was landing from the opposite direction. The Lightning pilot pulled back on his stick and neatly skipped over the big Liberator.

Another P-38 pilot, Lieutenant Joseph Price, trying to land on the Saidor strip with one engine dead from lack of fuel, was startled to hear from the control tower that an A-20 Havoc, also on its final approach, was directly beneath him. Price veered sideways, somehow kept the staggering Lightning from rolling over onto its back and then, crashing through underbrush and mud, bellied in next to the strip, landing parallel to the Havoc. Price calmly removed his gear from the cockpit and stood on the wing for a moment; then he passed out, overcome by the strain.

Not all were so lucky. A number of pilots, disoriented in the fog, spiraled into the jungle. The precise toll was not known for a day or so. That night Kenney counted no fewer than 70 planes not yet heard from, but some of these turned up in various places and in different states of damage. The final cost was 32 crewmen and 31 aircraft. But the Fifth had taken out Hollandia. When the invading Allied troops moved in on April 22 and overran the airstrips, they counted 340 wrecked Japanese aircraft.

With Rabaul dismantled, Wewak wrecked and bypassed, and Hollandia with its four Japanese-built airfields in the hands of Mac-

An A-20 Havoc bursts out of the smoke after bombing oil tanks on the Dutch East Indies island of Ceram. The raid helped sever Japan's vital fuel line. In 1944, the Dutch East Indies supplied Japan with more than 85 per cent of its aviation fuel and more than 75 per cent of its fuel oil.

Arthur's force, Kenney's kids kept moving westward along the northern New Guinea coast, Gloucesterizing the enemy strongholds on the offshore islands of Wakde, Biak and Numfor, and then building more airfields from which to attack Sansapor on the far western end of New Guinea. From there the Fifth's big bombers, now joined by those of the equally peripatetic Thirteenth, flew 2,000-mile round-trip missions to hit Japanese-controlled oil refineries at Balikpapan on the Borneo coast and also made less exhausting runs to the island of Morotai between New Guinea and the Philippines, a major stepping-stone for MacArthur's advance.

In October of 1944, Kenney and his Fifth made the enormous 1,000-mile leap from New Guinea to Leyte in the Philippines. In December, the Fifth once again constructed new fields; from them it could attack the Japanese air bases on Luzon—bases with such familiar names as Clark and Nichols—and disrupt Japanese shipping along the China coast.

The long, exhausting push from Port Moresby to Luzon was a tri-

During the reconquest of the Philippines in 1945, paratroops drop from a C-47 transport (center) on the island fortress of Corregidor in Manila Bay. B-24s and A-20 attack bombers had hammered Corregidor's defenses with 3,128 tons of bombs for almost a month.

of Kearby's flight, Captain William Dunham, saw that an Oscar was on his leader's tail. Dunham turned into the Oscar and "made a head-on pass. He broke his attack and turned into me. As he passed me his canopy flew off and he crashed into the hills." But so did Kearby. The Oscar apparently had poured a burst into Kearby's cockpit from close range and Kearby's P-47 plunged straight down. At his death, Kearby's log showed 24 aerial victories.

Thomas Lynch was shot down while flying on a two-man sweep with Richard Bong, who became the War's leading American ace *(pages 144-149)*. Although ordered to desk jobs by Kenney, who feared they were both too reckless, Lynch and Bong continued to fly, either tagging along with an active squadron or going off on their own. On March 9, 1944, Bong and Lynch set out on a two-man hunt over New Guinea. Bong later recalled that he and Lynch were on a routine sweep when they spotted three Japanese luggers "flubbing around in the water off the coast. It looked perfect for a strafing pass and it appeared as if there were fuel barrels on the ships' decks.

"Tom led us down and must have been going a good 300 miles an hour. I didn't see any kind of ack-ack and the run was easy—we were only going to make one pass. I was following Tom and when we pulled up I suddenly noticed his right propeller fly off and his engine start smoking. Tom made for the nearest shore and just as he approached it he bailed out. Almost right away, his plane exploded. And that's the last I ever saw of him."

That sweep, Bong said, "cost me one of my best friends and it cost the Air Force one of its best combat pilots." Lynch's final official score was 20 enemy planes.

Bong himself was eventually to shoot down 40 Japanese planes, the highest total in the theater. The only fighter pilot to threaten Bong's record was Major Thomas B. McGuire, who was 23 at the time he arrived in the Pacific in the spring of 1943. Although an extraordinary pilot, McGuire seemed fated to remain eight behind Bong's score. "I'll bet," he once said to Kenney, "when this war is over, they'll call me Eight-Behind McGuire."

The Bong-McGuire rivalry continued through the New Guinea campaign and into the Philippines. By then Bong was supposed to be instructing new arrivals in air gunnery and he had been told not to tangle with the Japanese except in self-defense. He was forced to defend himself often, however, and continued to run up his score. IN ACCORDANCE WITH MY INSTRUCTIONS, the impish Kenney wired Hap Arnold, MAJOR RICHARD BONG IS TRYING TO BE CAREFUL, but the Japa-

Shady Lady, a Twentieth Air Force B-29, wears the saucy nose art typical of many U.S. bombers during the War. Competition among crews to display the most titillating emblems led some commanders in the European theater to censor the images.

nese, he added, WON'T DO THEIR PART. Kenney eventually ordered Bong out of combat and sent him home.

He also grounded McGuire, who by that time had truly narrowed the gap with a score of 38. But McGuire would not stay grounded and, in company with Major Jack Rittmayer, a visitor from the Thirteenth Air Force, led a sweep by four P-38s over Negros Island, to the west of Leyte, on January 7, 1945. The two veterans were taking two new arrivals on a routine mission.

When an Oscar got on Rittmayer's tail, McGuire committed several errors he had consistently warned his student pilots against. He forgot to drop his wing tanks, he attempted to take on an Oscar too near the ground and he tried to make a tight turn at low speed to get on the tail of the Japanese plane. McGuire's P-38 shuddered for a moment, stalled and plummeted to the ground. An orange ball of flame bloomed out of the green jungle. McGuire was awarded the Medal of Honor posthumously for an escort mission he had led two weeks before. His final tally remained 38.

It had seemed a wonderful game, but all of Bong's major rivals—Lynch, Kearby and McGuire—were killed in action. Bong himself was killed during the summer of 1945 while test-flying the second U.S. jet aircraft, the Shooting Star.

As the air and ground forces got closer to Japan itself, General Arnold began to deploy a new plane in the Far East, the long-awaited Boeing B-29 Superfortress. Arnold and other high-ranking strategists had concluded that the B-17s and B-24s could finish the air war in Europe. The B-29s, placed under a new command, the Twentieth Air Force, would be reserved for the conflict in Asia.

By far the largest bomber produced during World War II, the B-29 weighed twice as much as its Boeing-built predecessor, the B-17, and could carry twice the bombload. Its four huge Wright engines provided 4,000 more horsepower than the Fort's engines. It could fly almost 70 miles an hour faster and its maximum range was almost double that of the B-17—4,200 miles.

The B-29 was also an innovational aircraft. Sections of its smooth, cylindrical fuselage were pressurized so that the crew could work without oxygen equipment and bulky flight gear. It also incorporated a centralized gun-control system in which a set of computers located in the belly of the plane helped the gunners calculate an enemy fighter's angle and speed of attack, making the fire of the plane's twelve .50-caliber machine guns far more deadly than the defensive armament on previous bombers. Some models had a 20-millimeter cannon in the tail.

General Arnold's initial plan was to raid Japan with B-29s flying from airfields near Chengtu in a part of China controlled by the friendly forces of Generalissimo Chiang Kai-shek. When the first production models began to roll off U.S. assembly lines in early 1944, one hundred fifty of them, commanded by Brigadier General Kenneth Wolfe, set off for

Asia, flying an 11,530-mile route from Kansas to Brazil, across the southern Atlantic to Marrakesh in Morocco and thence via Cairo and Karachi to Calcutta, India. From there the giant planes flew over the Himalayas into China.

The plan proved unworkable. Chiang had no reserves of aviation fuel; every gallon used by the B-29s, and every pound of bombs, had to be hauled some 1,000 miles by air over the Himalayas, the so-called Hump, into China. Six cargo planes loaded with drums of gasoline had to brave the Hump to supply enough fuel to send just one B-29 on a single raid. Chinese laborers by the thousands had pounded rock to construct the long runways needed by the big bombers, but the insuperable supply problems prevented General Wolfe from mounting either large or effective raids. Wolfe was soon relieved by an impatient Arnold and replaced on August 29 by Curtis LeMay, who had proved to be an effective commander with the Eighth Air Force in England.

Even the tough, demanding LeMay could do little to rectify the situation. One of his worst problems was the B-29 itself. Rushed into production without the usual exhaustive testing period, the aircraft was plagued by an inordinate number of mechanical bugs. The engines overheated, LeMay recalled, and "cylinder heads often blew out the moment an engine started turning over, ignition was faulty, oil leaked excessively, fuel transfer systems gave endless trouble. About four missions a month was the best we could do out of China, and sometimes we didn't even manage that."

The conquest of Guam, Saipan and Tinian in the Marianas chain of the western Pacific by Marine and Army units during the late summer and fall of 1944 provided suitable airfields for the B-29s. The islands could be supplied with bombs and fuel by Navy cargo ships, and they were only some 1,500 miles southeast of Japan, well within B-29 range.

Some 500 Chinese laborers—men and women alike—strain to pull a 10-ton concrete roller over a bed of mud, stone and gravel to pack a runway at an American airstrip near Chengtu. Since there were no bulldozers available in China, the Fourteenth Air Force depended on manpower to build its bases.

The Seventh Air Force, which helped in the conquest, had moved toward Japan, as the air crews disgustedly said, via "one damned island after another," cooperating with the Navy in attacks on Tarawa in the Gilberts and Kwajalein in the Marshalls before softening up the Marianas for amphibious invasions.

Even before the Marines had flushed out the last of the Marianas' stubborn Japanese defenders, engineers began to bulldoze airstrips. The first Superfort touched down on a not-quite-finished runway on Saipan on October 12, 1944, carrying Brigadier General Haywood S. Hansell, who would head the newly formed XXI Bomber Command, part of the Twentieth Air Force. Fourteen B-29s flew the first mission from the Marianas on October 28, bombing the Japanese stronghold on Truk. On November 24 Tokyo saw its first American bombers since Doolittle's B-25s, two and one half years before.

But Hansell's missions, like LeMay's, were not effective. Cloudy Japanese weather made it difficult to use the B-29 as it was designed to be used—as a very high altitude heavy. Over Japan at bombing altitudes of 25,000 feet and up the Superforts also encountered the ferocious Pacific jet stream. Heading into it, the planes virtually stood still; going downwind, they were whisked over the target. Either way, bombing accuracy suffered. Hansell echoed LeMay's gripes about the afflictions that plagued the B-29 despite modifications and corrections. "The engines of the B-29 had developed a very mean tendency to swallow valves and catch fire," he noted. "The magnesium crank cases burned with a fury that defied all efforts to put them out."

Handicapped by these mechanical problems, plus the wind and cloudy weather over Japan, XXI Bomber Command was not performing up to Arnold's expectations. Again Arnold called in LeMay, who was told, in effect, get results with the B-29 or you will be fired.

LeMay moved into his new job as head of XXI Bomber Command on January 20, 1945. Initially applying the same precision daylight bombardment tactics that Hansell had employed, LeMay wrought no miracles. He began to consider alternatives. He knew that the Japanese, during their long invasion of China, had dropped incendiary bombs on a number of Chinese cities with dreadful effect and he knew that Japanese cities were just as flammable. He also knew that Japan's major industries were located in its cities and that clustered around the factories were dozens or hundreds of workshops, often in private dwellings, that turned out parts and other war materials.

LeMay struggled with his conscience for several weeks. Should he use incendiaries? He did not want to abandon precision attacks for indiscriminate bombing of civilian centers, but if he did not get better results, the War might drag on for years and 500,000 to a million men would be killed invading Japan.

Finally in early March LeMay made up his mind to use incendiaries—both magnesium bombs that burned with a white heat and others filled with highly flammable oil. He also decided that the

Pilots from the 23rd Fighter Group, an offshoot of Claire Chennault's American Volunteer Group in China, radiate pride after intercepting 41 Japanese planes attacking an American air base at Kunming. Known as the Flying Tigers, the AVG popularized the shark's-mouth motif on the P-40s they flew.

B-29s would attack by night from as low as 5,000 feet; this would allow them to get under the jet stream and the persistent cloud cover. Some of LeMay's group commanders objected that Japanese antiaircraft guns would chew the formations to bits. But LeMay was willing to risk his force on the gamble that Japanese low-altitude gunfire would prove far inferior to the German. Japanese antiaircraft gunnery had never been very effective during the island campaigns. Perhaps it would be no better over Tokyo.

There were other advantages in low-level attack. Not having to climb to 30,000 feet would reduce the strain on the temperamental engines and the planes would consume less fuel. Therefore they could carry larger bombloads.

LeMay chose the night of March 9-10 for the first of the incendiary raids. A total of 334 Superforts left Guam, Saipan and Tinian in the late afternoon for Tokyo, each carrying 12,000 pounds of fire bombs.

Shortly after midnight the leading wave of B-29s reached Tokyo and, flying below the cloud cover, found the visibility good. It was easy for the bombardiers to locate the target. Tokyo lies at the head of easily recognized Tokyo Bay, and the Sumida River bisects the city. Two advance formations of B-29s crisscrossed the city, dropping fire bombs at intervals of 100 feet. When they were finished, a huge blazing X could be seen, marking a part of Tokyo crowded with industries—and with wood, plaster and bamboo dwellings.

The rest of the B-29s came in at altitudes between 4,900 and 9,200 feet and dropped their bombs on the brilliantly marked target area. Brigadier General Thomas S. Powers, air commander of the raid, reported by radio to LeMay, who was anxiously waiting on Guam: "Bombing the target visually. Large fires observed. Flak moderate. Fighter opposition nil." LeMay had won his gamble—the low-level bombing had worked and he had not lost his force. In fact only 14 of the B-29s went down, most of them to sporadic antiaircraft fire. Five crews were subsequently picked up from the Pacific, where they had crash-landed.

For the Japanese this first fire raid was a major catastrophe. The fires quickly raged out of control. The heat rose to 1,800° F. Violent updrafts from the flames, LeMay wrote, "bounced our planes into the sky like ping-pong balls"; some of these updrafts were evident up to 15,000 feet. Down below about 16 square miles of Tokyo were burning, including 22 industrial plants. One fourth of all the city's buildings, some 267,000 structures, went up in flames. The official death toll was 83,793, with another 40,918 injured, but it seems certain that the number of dead was actually much higher. Many thousands were drowned in the Sumida River trying to escape the fierce heat, and many bodies were never recovered. Others were burned to ash.

LeMay immediately realized that, as he reported to Arnold, "the destruction of Japan's ability to wage war lies within the capability of this command." He quickly followed the Tokyo attack with a 10-day fire

Perched on coral hardstands and surrounded by miles of taxi strips, B-29 Superforts stretch along both sides of the two 8,500-foot runways at North Field, Guam. The ground traffic control system was called the "Miracle of the Marianas."

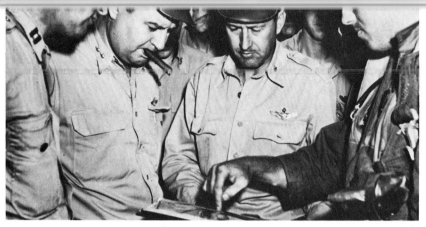

Cigar in mouth, Major General Curtis LeMay of XXI Bomber Command discusses strategy with Brigadier General Thomas Powers, on his left. When high-altitude daylight bombing proved ineffective, LeMay dispatched Powers' Mariana-based B-29s on a series of low-level night incendiary attacks on Japan's industrial cities.

blitz on other Japanese cities; Osaka, Kobe and Nagoya suffered the same fate as Tokyo. Then LeMay stopped: He had exhausted his stock of incendiaries.

After a three-week pause, during which the Navy shipped thousands of tons of bombs to the Marianas, the B-29s revisited Tokyo, putting down more than 2,100 tons of bombs, the most to date. Another 11 square miles of buildings were razed. By that time the Japanese people were fleeing from their cities—what was left of them—and finding refuge in the hills. Tokyo's population went from five million to two and a third million. The life of the city and its remaining industries came to a virtual halt.

The Japanese air defenses shot down a few marauding B-29s but were powerless to stop the devastating raids. Japanese antiaircraft gunnery, lacking radar aids, was not on a par with the German; although night fighters occasionally challenged the B-29s, they seldom made effective interception.

While bomber losses to the Japanese were relatively light, weather and mechanical failure took a far heavier toll. The Tokyo run was almost twice the length of the deepest penetrations into Germany, and virtually the entire journey was over water. The bombers generally left the Marianas about 5:30 in the evening and were over Japan at midnight or 1 o'clock; the crews often saw the sun rising before they set down on their home fields. When the Marines, in one of the fiercest battles of the War, captured the tiny island of Iwo Jima, halfway between the Marianas and Japan, malfunctioning B-29s at last had a place to make emergency landings. Before the War ended, 2,251 B-29s suffering from battle damage or mechanical problems made it safely to Iwo.

Every sign indicated that Japan was hopelessly beaten. While the

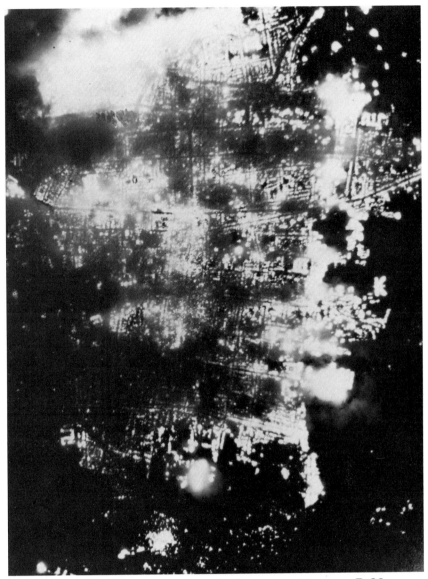

In the most destructive fire raid of the War against Japan, the aluminum-producing city of Toyama goes up in flames under a hail of incendiary bombs. Japan's cities, with their houses of paper and wood, "caught fire like a forest of pine trees," said one B-29 pilot.

main force of B-29s continued to raid Japanese cities, one B-29 group dropped mines in Japan's harbors and home waters. What was left of Japan's merchant fleet was immobilized and raw materials for Japan's war industries ceased to flow into the few industrial plants that were still functioning. But the diehards in the Japanese government remained determined to fight on. If the United States were forced to invade Japan, they felt, the terrible cost in lives would lead the Americans to seek a negotiated peace. Orders went out that every Japanese man between the ages of 15 and 60 and all women aged 17 to 40 would meet the invaders at the beaches with sharpened bamboo poles. Allied peace feelers were rejected.

In June and July a new unit, called the 509th Composite Group, flew into North Field on Tinian in 15 modified Superforts with redesigned bomb bays, which the crew members refused to discuss with anyone. The 509th, commanded by Colonel Paul W. Tibbets, a veteran of the air war in Europe, had trained for secrecy's sake at a remote desert air

base in Utah. None of the men aside from Tibbets had any inkling of
what they were training to do, for all had been told to keep their mouths
shut. This was even more true of their three months on Tinian in the
Marianas. There they did not participate in regular missions but instead made
mysterious practice flights.

off from Tinian and headed for Hiroshima, Kokura and Nagasaki, three
cities that had so far escaped bombing. They were to report which of the
cities had the best visibility.

About one hour later Colonel Tibbets took off in the *Enola Gay*, a
B-29 named after his mother, and headed for Japan. Aboard was a
long, thin metal cylinder weighing 9,000 pounds—the uranium bomb
called Little Boy. As the *Enola Gay* flew toward Japan, a Navy officer,
Captain William Parsons, who was an ordnance expert, inserted the last
key components in the bomb. It had not been live on takeoff, since B-
29s had a history of engine failure while lifting. With the *Enola Gay* went
two other B-29s carrying observers, scientific instruments and cameras.
The weather planes soon checked in, informing Tibbets that Hiroshima
was relatively free of clouds.

At 8:15 a.m. Little Boy was toggled free from 31,600 feet. Tibbets
immediately put the *Enola Gay* into a fast, diving turn to get away from
the coming explosion. The bomb created an immense fireball, the temperature at its center about 50 million° C., some three times greater than
the estimated heat at the center of the sun. The explosion exerted a
pressure of hundreds of thousands of tons to the square inch. The B-29
crews saw a soon-to-be-famous cloud "shaped like a mushroom" rise
"to 20,000 feet in one minute."

It was immediately evident to some in the Japanese government that
continued resistance was out of the question. On August 8 Foreign
Minister Shigenori Togo met with Emperor Hirohito and they agreed to
sue for peace at once. Still it was not until the next day that the Supreme
Council meeting was held. The delay was tragic.

At precisely 11:01 a.m., while the Japanese government was discuss-
ing peace terms, Major Charles W. Sweeney—flying a B-29 called
Bock's Car after the plane's regular pilot, Captain Frederick Bock—
completed his bomb run and the plutonium bomb, Fat Man, began its
fall toward the center of Nagasaki. The blast, Sweeney reported, made it
feel as though his B-29 "were being beaten by a telegraph pole."

So were the Japanese vanquished, even though some diehards attempted to hold out. The intervention of the Emperor himself finally
brought about unconditional surrender on August 15. The ceremony
took place on the deck of the U.S.S. *Missouri* on September 2, 1945.
Among those present was General Doolittle, who later appraised with
characteristic succinctness the contribution of the Superfortress to the
victory. "The Navy had the transport to make the invasion of Japan
possible," he said, "the ground forces had the power to make it possible; and the B-29 made it unnecessary."　　　　　　　　　　～～

The crew of the Enola Gay assembles after dropping the atomic bomb on Hiroshima. Not until they were in the air did the pilot, Colonel Paul Tibbets (standing, center), tell them of their mission.

The devastated center of Hiroshima bears mute testimony to the lethal power of Little Boy (inset), the bomb that killed 80,000 people.

Acknowledgments

The index for this book was prepared by Gale... Maggiore Esercito. **In Sweden:** Malmo—Bertil... (Ret.); Mary Lou Giernes, Center for Military...

Roger de Ruffray, Deputy Director, Colonel Pierre Willefert, Curator, Musée de l'Air. **In Great Britain:** London—Michael Hollingshead, Popperfoto; Edward Hine, Alan Williams, Imperial War Museum; Marjorie Willis, BBC Hulton Picture Library. **In Holland:** Amsterdam—Rijksinstituut voor Oorlogsdocumentatie; Leidschendam—Bart M. Rijnhout; Sittard—Bert Poels; Soesterberg— Dutch Airforce Museum. **In Italy:** Rome— Colonel Oreste Bovio, Ufficio Storico, Stato

Schneide, Jay Spencer, Robert van der Linden, National Air and Space Museum; Alice Price, the Pentagon; Massachusetts—Marvin Lubner; Minnesota—Patricia Stevens; Nebraska— Edward L. Homze, University of Nebraska; New York—Mike Jackson, *Army Times* Publishing Co.; Ohio—Catherine E. Cassity, Wright-Patterson Air Force Base; Royal D. Frey; Robert T. O'Brien; Texas—John Ilfrey; Virginia—Janice King, Colonel Eric Solander, Air Force Office of Public Affairs; General Benjamin O. Davis Jr.

Particularly useful sources of information and quotations used in this volume were: *The Army Air Forces in World War II* by Wesley F. Craven and James L. Cate, eds., 7 vols., University of Chicago Press, 1948-1958; *General Kenney Reports: A Personal History of the Pacific War* by General George C. Kenney, Duell, Sloan and Pearce, 1949; *The Mighty Eighth, Units, Men and Machines* by Roger A. Freeman, Doubleday, 1970; *The 9th Air Force in World War II* by Kenn C. Rust, Aero, 1970.

Bibliography

Books

Arnold, H. H., *Global Mission*. Harper & Brothers, 1949.

Birdsall, Steve:
Flying Buccaneers: The Illustrated Story of Kenney's Fifth Air Force. Doubleday, 1977.
Log of the Liberators: An Illustrated History of the B-24. Doubleday, 1973.
Saga of the Superfortress: The Dramatic Story of the B-29 and the Twentieth Air Force. Doubleday, 1980.

Brereton, Lewis H., *The Brereton Diaries: The War in the Air in the Pacific, Middle East and Europe, 3 October 1941-8 May 1945*. William Morrow, 1946.

Carter, Kit C., and Robert Mueller, eds., *The Army Air Forces in World War II: Combat Chronology 1941-1945*. U.S. Government Printing Office, 1973.

Craven, Wesley F., and James L. Cate, eds., *The Army Air Forces in World War II*. 7 vols. University of Chicago Press, 1948-1958.

Cunningham, William Glenn, *The Aircraft Industry: A Study in Industrial Location*. Lorrin L. Morrison, 1951.

Dank, Milton, *The Glider Gang: An Eyewitness History of World War II Glider Combat*. London: Cassell, 1978.

Dugan, James, and Carroll Stewart, *Ploesti: The Great Ground-Air Battle of 1 August 1943*. Random House, 1962.

Edmonds, Walter D., *They Fought With What They Had*. Little, Brown, 1951.

Esposito, Colonel Vincent J., ed., *The West Point Atlas of American Wars, Vol. 2, 1900-1953*. Frederick A. Praeger, 1959.

Freeman, Roger A.:
The Mighty Eighth: Units, Men and Machines. Doubleday, 1970.
Thunderbolt: A documentary history of the Republic P-47. Charles Scribner's Sons, 1979.

Glines, Carroll V., *Doolittle's Tokyo Raiders*. D. Van Nostrand, 1964.

Goldberg, Alfred, ed., *A History of the United States Air Force*. Arno Press, 1974.

Green, William:
Famous Bombers of the Second World War. Doubleday, 1959.
Famous Fighters of the Second World War. Hanover House, 1960.

Gropman, Alan L., *The Air Force Integrates, 1945-1964*. U.S. Government Printing Office, 1978.

Gurney, Gene, *The War in the Air: a pictorial history of World War II Air Forces in combat*. Bonanza Books, 1962.

Hall, Grover C., Jr., *1000 Destroyed: The Life and Times of the 4th Fighter Group*. Aero, 1946.

Haugland, Vern, *The AAF Against Japan*. Harper & Brothers, 1948.

Hess, William N., ed., *The American Fighter Aces Album*. Taylor Publishing, 1978.

Impact: The Army Air Forces' Confidential Picture History of World War II. 8 vols. James Parton and Company, 1980.

Jablonski, Edward:
Airwar. Doubleday, 1971.
Flying Fortress: The Illustrated Biography of the B-17s and the Men Who Flew Them. Doubleday, 1965.

Kenney, General George C.:
Dick Bong: Ace of Aces. Zenger Publishing Co., 1960.
General Kenney Reports: A Personal History of the Pacific War. Duell, Sloan and Pearce, 1949.

Lee, Ulysses, *The Employment of Negro Troops*. U.S. Government Printing Office, 1970.

LeMay, General Curtis E., and MacKinlay Kantor, *My Story: Mission with LeMay*. Doubleday, 1965.

Life's Picture History of World War II. Time Inc., 1950.

Lord, Walter, *Day of Infamy*. Henry Holt, 1957.

Osur, Alan M., *Blacks in the Army Air Forces during World War II: The Problem of Race Relations*. U.S. Government Printing Office, 1941.

Peaslee, Budd J., *Heritage of Valor: The Eighth Air Force in World War II*. J. B. Lippincott, 1964.

Robertson, Bruce, ed., *United States Army and Air Force Fighters 1916-1961*. Aero, 1961.

Rose, Robert A., *Lonely Eagles: The story of America's black air force in World War II*. Tuskegee Airmen Inc., 1976.

Rust, Kenn C.:
Eighth Air Force Story. Historical Aviation Album, 1978.
Fifteenth Air Force Story. Historical Aviation Album, 1976.
Fifth Air Force Story. Historical Aviation Album, 1973.
The 9th Air Force in World War II. Aero, 1970.

Sunderman, James F., ed., *World War II in the Air: Europe*. Franklin Watts, 1963.

Thomas, Gordon, and Max Morgan Witts, *Enola Gay*. Stein and Day, 1977.

Thomas, Lowell, and Edward Jablonski, *Doolittle: A Biography*. Doubleday, 1976.

Titler, Dale, *Wings of Mystery: True Stories of Aviation History*. Dodd Mead, 1981.

Toliver, Raymond F., and Trevor J. Constable, *Fighter Aces of the U.S.A.* Aero, 1979.

Tute, Warren, John Costello and Terry Hughes, *D-Day*. Macmillan, 1974.

Wragg, David W., ed., *A Dictionary of Aviation*. Frederick Fell, 1973.

Young, Brigadier Peter, ed., *Atlas of the Second World War*. Berkley Publishing, 1974.

Picture credits

The sources for the illustrations in this book are listed below. Credits from left to right are separated by semicolons; from top to bottom they are separated by dashes.
Endpaper (and cover detail, regular edition): Painting by R. G. Smith. 6, 7: *B-24s on Ploesti Raid* by Standley Dersch, courtesy U.S. Air Force Art Collection. 8, 9: *War Hawks at Amchitka* by Ogden Pleissner, courtesy U.S. Army. 10, 11: *Supply Line in China* by Loren R. Fisher, courtesy U.S. Air Force Art Collection. 12, 13: *B-25 On a Mission* by Robert Laessig, courtesy U.S. Air Force Art Collection. 14, 15: *War and Peace* by Peter Hurd, courtesy U.S. Army. 16, 17: U.S. Air Force Photo. 18: National Archives No. 80-G-32915. 21: U.S. Air Force Photo. 22: Associated Press, courtesy Imperial War Museum, London. 23: U.S. Army Photo No. SC127184—Margaret Bourke-White for *Life* (2); U.S. Air Force Photo. 25: *Air Raid on Clark Field* by K. Sato, courtesy U.S. Air Force Art Collection. 26: U.S. Air Force Photo. 28: Courtesy Lockheed-California Company. 29: J. R. Eyerman for *Life*—courtesy Lockheed-California Company. 30, 31: U.S. Air Force Photo, courtesy Edward Jablonski—Wide World: 32. National Air and Space Museum,

Smithsonian Institution. 36, 37: U.S. Air Force Photo, courtesy Edward Jablonski (2); U.S. Air Force Photo. 38: U.S. Air Force Photo. 39: U.S. Army Photo No. SC168885. 40-43: U.S. Air Force Photos. 44: U.S. Air Force Photo—U.S. Air Force Museum. 45: U.S. Air Force Museum. 46: Peter Stackpole for *Life*—U.S. Air Force Photo. 47: U.S. Air Force Photo—U.S. Air Force Museum. 48, 49: U.S. Air Force Photo. 50: William Vandivert for *Life*—U.S. Air Force Photo. 51: U.S. Air Force Photo (2)—U.S. Air Force Museum. 52: Photoworld/FPG. 55: U.S. Air Force Photo, courtesy Edward Jablonski. 57: U.S. Air Force Photo. 58: Wide World. 59: Photo Trends. 60, 61: Frank Schershel for *Life*. 62-64: Popperfoto, London. 66: Courtesy the Boeing Company Archives. 68, 69: U.S. Air Force Photos. 70, 71: Staatliche Landesbildstelle, Hamburg. 74, 75: UPI. 76: Courtesy Alex Waranka, UPI. 77: Wide World. 80-87: Margaret Bourke-White for *Life*. 88-92: U.S. Air Force Photos. 94: U.S. Air Force Photo, courtesy Edward Jablonski; Joe Oravec, courtesy Edward Jablonski; U.S. Air Force Photo. 95: Popperfoto, London. 97: Associated Press, London. 98: U.S. Air Force Photo. 100, 101: U.S. Air Force Photo—drawing by Bill Hezlep. 105:

U.S. Air Force Photo. 106-111: Drawings by John Amendola. 112-122: U.S. Air Force Photos. 125: Dmitri Kessel, courtesy Musée des Deux Guerres Mondiales-B.D.I.C. (Universités de Paris), Inc.. 126, 127: U.S. Army Photo No. SC190293. 129: U.S. Air Force Photo. 130-133: Drawings by John Batchelor. 136-143: U.S. Air Force Photos. 144: Courtesy of the Bong family. 145: Courtesy of the Bong family (2)—U.S. Air Force Photo, from *Dick Bong, Ace of Aces*, by General George C. Kenney, courtesy Zenger Publishing Co., Inc.; U.S. Air Force Photo. 146, 147: Courtesy of the Bong family. 148: Courtesy of the Bong family; Wide World—courtesy of the Bong family. 149: U.S. Air Force Photo—courtesy of the Bong family. 150, 151: U.S. Air Force Photo, courtesy Edward Jablonski. 155: Painting by Shugaku Homma, courtesy U.S. Navy—Terry Gwynn-Jones. 156, 157: U.S. Air Force Photo, courtesy Edward Jablonski. 160: U.S. Air Force Photo. 162: U.S. Air Force Photo. 164: U.S. Air Force Photo, courtesy Edward Jablonski. 165: U.S. Air Force Photo. 166: J. R. Eyerman for *Life*. 168: Imperial War Museum, courtesy Alfred Price, London. 169: U.S. Air Force Photo. 170, 171: U.S. Air Force Photo.

Index